Tourette Syndrome

A Practical Guide for Teachers, Parents and Carers

Amber Carroll and Mary Robertson

David Fulton Publishers
London

David Fulton Publishers Ltd
Ormond House, 26–27 Boswell Street, London WC1N 3JD
www.fultonpublishers.co.uk

First published in Great Britain by David Fulton Publishers 2000

British Library Cataloguing in Publication Data
A catalogue record for this book is available from the British Library

ISBN 1–85346–656–5

Typeset by Textype Typesetters, Cambridge
Printed in Great Britain by Bell and Bain Ltd, Glasgow

Contents

Acknowledgements

We would like to thank Dr Jeremy Stern and Miss Gabrielle Stern for reading and commenting on drafts of this work.

Abbreviations Used in This Book

ADHD	Attention Deficit Hyperactivity Disorder
CBT	Cognitive Behaviour Therapy
CD	Conduct Disorder
CMT	Chronic Motor Tic disorder
CVT	Chronic Vocal Tic disorder
DCI	Diagnostic Confidence Index
DSM	Diagnostic and Statistical Manual (of the American Psychiatric Association)
EBD	Emotional and Behavioural Difficulties
ECG	ElectroCardioGram
ENT	Ear Nose and Throat
EPSE	ExtraPyramidal Side Effects
EWS	Education Welfare Service
GAD	Generalised Anxiety Disorder
HD	Huntington's Disease
ICT	Information and Communication Technology
IEP	Individual Education Plan
LD	Learning Disabled
LSA	Learning Support Assistant
MOVES	Motor tic Obsessions and compulsions Vocal tic Evaluation Survey
MSA	Midday Supervisory Assistant
NASEN	National Association for Special Educational Needs
NHIS	National Hospital Interview Schedule
NHSS	National Healthy School Standard
NOSI	Non Obscene Socially Inappropriate behaviours
OCB	Obsessive Compulsive Behaviours
OCD	Obsessive Compulsive Disorder
ODD	Oppositional Defiant Disorder
OT	Occupational Therapy
PANDAS	Paediatric Autoimmune Neuropsychiatric Disorders associated with group A beta-heamolytic Streptococcal infection
PIQ	Performance Intelligence Quotient

PKU	PhenylKetonUria
PSHE	Personal Social and Health Education
PSP	Pastoral Support Programme
RoA	Record of Achievement
SEN	Special Educational Needs
SENCO	Special Educational Needs Co-Ordinator
SIB	Self Injurious Behaviour
SMT	Senior Management Team
SSSRI	Selective Serotonin Reuptake Inhibitor
TCA	TriCyclic Antidepressant
TSSS	Tourette Syndrome Severity Scale
TTD	Transient Tic Disorder
TTS	Tardive Tourette Syndrome
VIQ	Verbal Intelligence Quotient
VMI	VisuoMotor Integration
WAIS	Wechsler Adult Intelligence Scales
WD	Wilson's Disease
WISC	Wechsler Intelligence Scales for Children
YGTSS	Yale Global Tic Severity Scale
YOT	Youth Offending Team

Introduction

It is most helpful when teachers, like clinicians view the child as a whole person, develop a broad view of a pupil's overall academic and social functioning, and avoid the temptation to fix upon target symptoms.

(Cohen *et al.* 1992)

Gilles de la Tourette Syndrome (TS) is a developmental neuropsychiatric disorder, which is suggested to be genetic/inherited and is now generally recognised to be one of the main medical causes of tics (also called 'habits', 'twitches' or 'mannerisms') in children and young people.

The aim of this book is to provide information about and insights into TS, and how individuals with TS can be supported in school to maximise their potential, however mild, moderate or severe their symptoms. The first half of the book examines TS to provide the teachers and others involved in education with more information about the disorder. The second half provides strategies for supporting the pupil with TS in schools.

While much of the medical literature is devoted to individuals who have moderate or severe TS, we would like to make the point at the outset that most children with TS probably have it in a mild, uncomplicated or 'pure' form, are unknown to doctors or other health professionals, and can be educated in mainstream schools. These youngsters' symptoms may well be noticed first by the teacher, who may decide to do nothing, or can suggest to the parents a referral to a doctor, discuss the symptoms with the head teacher, the school's educational psychologist or special educational needs coordinator (SENCO), or take any other appropriate action. The symptoms of these pupils with uncomplicated TS are often so mild that probably neither they nor their parents realise that they have tics or TS. They almost certainly do not consider their 'habits' a problem.

We look at the definitions of TS and tics, and discuss in some detail how common tics and TS are, many of the studies having been carried out in schools. TS is probably more common than was once recognised and in some cases pupils may require special educational assistance. We then discuss the diagnostic criteria and clinical characteristics of TS, illustrating the symptoms and giving examples, and briefly describe assessment schedules used in the diagnosis or measurement of TS. The associated behaviours and conditions are addressed as they may well have an impact on schooling. Famous and successful people who reputedly have had TS are briefly discussed, and mention is made of TS in the popular literature.

Unless otherwise indicated, statements here about the definition of tics and clinical characteristics of TS will be taken from the *Diagnostic and Statistical Manual* (fourth edition) of the American Psychiatric Association (APA 1994) as well as from two thorough reviews authored by one of us (Robertson 1989; 1994). Basic information on the general psychiatric aspects will be adapted from a recently published psychiatric textbook co-authored by one of us (Katona and Robertson 2000) and from the APA (1994).

Chapter 1

Tics and Tourette Syndrome: An Introduction

> Tourette Syndrome is a model neuropsychiatric disorder that seems tantalizing in its simplicity . . . [but] is a very complex disorder, [which] is not just a disorder of tics: it is a disorder of sensations, and it has an internal life invisible to the external world.   (Swerdlow 1999)

The main symptoms of TS are tics. A tic is a sudden, rapid, recurrent, purposeless, non-rhythmic, involuntary motor movement (motor tic) or sound (vocal, phonic tic). Characteristically, tics are reduced during sleep. Tics may be simple or complex and include many examples, as can be seen in Table 1.

Definitions of tics

Childhood tics are common and have been reported to occur in approximately four per cent to 18 per cent of youngsters, with many studies finding tics in about 10 per cent of children. In nearly all studies, tics were more commonly found in boys than in girls (Robertson and Stern 2000). Tics have a variety of causes, but only some of these are causally (aetiologically) related to TS.

How common are tics?

At least two studies examining tics in children have involved teachers in the investigations. Thus, Fallon and Schwab-Stone (1992) surveyed teachers in Eastern Connecticut in the USA, who identified 10 per cent of children between the ages of six and 12 years as having tic behaviours. Mason *et al.* (1998) studied 13–14-year-old pupils in a mainstream secondary school in west Essex, UK for tics and TS. Questionnaires completed by parents, teachers and pupils, as well as classroom observations and interviews, undertaken by a psychologist, were employed to identify tics; 18 per cent were diagnosed as possibly having tics.

In one study investigating the incidence of tics in a population with severe learning difficulties between the ages of seven and 86 years, in the USA, tics were reported in 16.6 per cent of individuals (Long *et al.* 1998). In another study undertaken in pupils with special educational needs (SEN) in a single school district in California USA, tics were found in 28 per cent (Comings *et al.* 1990).

Table 1: Simple and complex tics

Common simple motor tics	Simple vocal tics
• excessive eye blinking	• repetitive throat clearing
• eye rolling	• grunting
• squinting	• sniffing
• nose twitching	• snorting
• mouth opening	• coughing
• facial grimacing (pulling faces)	
• head nodding (backwards or forwards)	*Complex vocal tics*
• flicking of the hair out of the eyes (as if the hair/fringe is too long)	• inappropriate fluctuations in the pitch of the voice
• inappropriate rapid tongue protrusion	• muttering under one's breath
• shoulder shrugging	• saying inappropriate words
• neck twisting or stretching	• making the sounds of certain animals, such as the quack of a
• both upper and lower limb jerking	duck or noise of a pig
	• coprolalia (inappropraite involuntary swearing)
Complex motor tics	• echolalia (copying what others say)
• facial gestures (such as inappropriate smiling)	
• jumping up and down	
• licking things	
• smelling things	
• squatting	
• abnormalities of gait (such as twirling and retracing steps)	
• feeling compelled to touch things (other people, objects, or dangerous or 'forbidden' objects)	

Tics are found in a substantial number of children, with 10 per cent being the most common figure in studies. It appears that tics may well also be more common in people with SEN, or in people with learning difficulties, although so far relatively few studies have been carried out.

How common is Tourette Syndrome?

Motor tics are common in children, occurring in about 10 per cent of children. Many of these children will have transient tic disorder or chronic motor tic disorder (see later), but some may well have TS.

Prior to the 1980s TS (in which both motor *and* vocal tics must be present, although not necessarily concurrently) was thought to be very rare indeed. In the early medical and scientific literature for many years, only isolated case reports were documented. Since then the generally accepted prevalence figure for TS has been between 5 per 10,000 (Bruun 1984) and 10 per 10,000 (Costello *et al.* 1996); i.e. no fewer than 25,000 to 50,000 individuals in the United Kingdom. In a well known International Registry published in 1973, only 174 TS cases were documented in the USA and only 53 in the UK (Abuzzahab and Anderson 1973). For reviews of early epidemiological studies of TS see Robertson (1989; 1994; 2000). Recent investigations have, however, indicated that TS may well be much more common than was once previously thought.

The following studies all investigated pupils at schools in both the USA and the UK. Some of the studies were conducted in mainstream schools, while others were undertaken in schools for children with SEN.

Two relatively recent studies in mainstream schools (one in the UK and one in the USA) found very similar results for the frequency of TS. The UK study was undertaken in a secondary school in west Essex. All pupils aged 13 to 14 years were studied and revealed a high frequency. Questionnaires as well as classroom observations and interviews were employed to identify TS. Five out of 166 pupils (2.9 per cent) satisfied criteria for definite/probable TS. Of importance is that all individuals identified had mild TS symptoms (Mason *et al.* 1998).

In another school study in Monroe County, New York, USA, 3 per cent of the 35 regular school pupils had TS (Kurlan *et al.* 1994). These studies could be criticised in that they both employed a small number of children (166 and 35 respectively), and were essentially pilot studies. However, they do make the point that TS is probably more common in school children than was once thought.

In studies of children with SEN, however, the prevalence of TS has been demonstrated to be substantially higher in three separate studies, two in the USA and one in the UK. In the first, already mentioned study in a single Californian school district, over 3000 pupils referred for psycho-educational assessment from three schools were studied. It was estimated that 12 per cent of all pupils in special education classes had TS (Comings *et al.* 1990). Another study examined over 30 children from special education classes in Monroe County, New York. Of the students with SEN, 26 per cent had definite or probable tics; about one-third with tics met criteria for TS (Kurlan *et al.* 1994). The third study was from west Essex in the UK and included over 80 pupils. Several groups of children were studied. These included pupils from a residential school for emotional and behavioural difficulties (EBD), children from a residential school for individuals with learning difficulties, 'problem' children and 'normal' children who were all pupils at a mainstream school. Of the pupils with EBD two-thirds were judged to have tics, compared to one quarter of pupils with learning difficulties, only 6 per cent of the 'problem' children, and none of the 'normal' mainstream children; the majority were judged to have TS (Eapen *et al.* 1997). Full details of these studies are described in Robertson (2000).

There have been several documentations from the USA suggesting an association between TS and autism. Recently in the UK, there have been two studies suggesting that TS is found frequently in youngsters with autism spectrum disorders (autism and Asperger's Syndrome). In a pilot study, TS was found to occur in eight per cent of 37 youngsters in the pilot study (Baron-Cohen *et al.* 1999a), while in a subsequent large scale study, TS was found in six per cent of 447 pupils (Baron-Cohen *et al.* 1999b).

All of this indicates that TS is now recognised as probably being more common than was previously thought, and that it may occur more often in children who have SEN, learning difficulties or disabilities and autistic spectrum disorders.

Where are individuals with Tourette Syndrome found?

TS is found in all cultures and most countries. It occurs three to four times more commonly in boys than in girls. TS is found in all social classes, although some studies have suggested that individuals with TS may well underachieve socially and, for instance, not attain their parents' social status and/or educational level. In a personal survey of many TS specialists worldwide (Robertson 1996), the only part of the world where there were no typical TS cases was Sub-Saharan Africa. There may be many reasons for this, including non-recognition and perceived relative unimportance of tics when many children are suffering from malnutrition and infectious diseases, but there may also be genetic factors, as some neurological disorders are not encountered in Sub-Saharan Africa. The symptoms of TS are similar irrespective of the country of origin.

A recent study by Freeman *et al.* (2000) has documented findings from 3,500 TS cases in 22 countries around the world including Argentina, Australia, Austria, Belgium, Brazil, Canada, Denmark, Germany, Hungary, Iceland, Israel, Italy, Japan, The Netherlands, Norway, People's Republic of China, Poland, South Africa, Sweden, Turkey, the United Kingdom and the United States of America.

The history of Tourette Syndrome

The first clear medical description of TS was made by a French neurologist, Jean Marc Gaspard Itard, in 1825, when he reported the case of a French noblewoman, the now famous Marquise de Dampierre. She developed motor tics at the age of seven, but later, at the time of her marriage, began to use swear words, which made her socially unacceptable in her circle, and she therefore had to live the rest of her life as a recluse. Dr Gilles de la Tourette subsequently in 1885, described nine cases of the disorder which went on to earn him eponymous fame.

The first reported case of TS in the UK may possibly have been Mary Hall of Gadsden, who was reported in 1663 by William Drage (Lees *et al.* 1984).

The history of TS is thoroughly covered by Kushner (1999) who describes the early years of TS in France, the psychological/psychoanalytical phase of causation, the 'infectious era', and finally on to modern times with the acknowledged clinical similarities and biological nature of the disorder.

TS is now well established as a medical condition and hundreds of publications about the various aspects of TS are published in the medical and scientific literature every year.

Dr Georges Albert Edouard Brutus Gilles de la Tourette (1857–1904) was a French neuropsychiatrist who worked at the famous Paris hospital, the Salpetrière. His life has been thoroughly documented by Lees (1986). Dr Gilles de la Tourette described nine cases of TS and highlighted the triad of multiple tics, echolalia (repeating sounds or words of other people) and coprolalia (the involuntary uttering of obscenities or blasphemous words), and which he suggested formed a distinct entity among movement disorders. Dr Gilles de la Tourette was famous for his study of hysteria, the medico-legal aspects of hypnotism, and his interest in neuropsychiatric therapeutics. In 1886 he obtained his doctoral thesis for his use of the method of using footprints to diagnose nervous disease! He also used the notorious 'suspension therapies' which were successful in the treatment of tabes dorsalis (a complication of syphilis), and he invented a vibratory helmet for use in neuralgia (nerve pain) and vertigo (the sensation of dizziness). He was eventually shot by a deluded and mentally ill patient, made a full recovery, but ironically died of general paralysis of the insane, also a complication of syphilis, in 1904 in Switzerland.

Gilles de la Tourette

In 1980, Bliss, a TS sufferer, wrote: 'I have been stalking this thing (TS) for over 35 years with a single minded determination to find something that would give me a clue, a direction, to the meaning of the problem'.

In the last two decades the important causes of TS have become well known as medical research has advanced and they include genetic influences, environmental influence and infections.

The causes of Tourette Syndrome

Genetics

By far the majority of TS cases are caused by genetic influences, and these may also be called primary or idiopathic TS. Although it is now generally agreed that TS is a genetically determined disorder, the precise mechanism of inheritance is as yet undetermined. The genetic background of TS has been recently reviewed by Robertson (2000). Many studies have suggested autosomal dominant inheritance (meaning that if a particular person had TS, each son/daughter would have a fifty-fifty chance of inheriting the gene). Many authorities now believe that an individual may inherit a vulnerability to what is now commonly called a 'spectrum disorder', which includes TS, OCB and, in some cases, a type of ADHD. However, there also may be genetic heterogeneity in TS which means that different genes may be involved in different families. In the human genetic make-up are proteins, genes and chromosomes, and many disorders have now been identified to be associated with a particular part of the gene and chromosome. To date there is no blood test for diagnosing TS.

In a large study recently published, two areas of interest in the human genome have been identified which may eventually be involved in the transmission of TS, and they are situated on chromosomes 4 and 8 (Tourette Syndrome Association International Consortium for Genetics 1999).

Environmental influences

Despite the fact that it is suggested that TS is genetically determined, other *perinatal factors* have also been proposed to be important in making an individual vulnerable to TS. These may include for example, very severe nausea and vomiting during pregnancy, the medications given for this vomiting, and birth complications such as the cord around the neck of the baby, 'yellow jaundice', prematurity (baby being born much too young), a caesarian section (delivery by caesarian operation), forceps delivery and a very prolonged labour (Robertson 2000). Forceps delivery, and foetal exposure to high levels of coffee, cigarettes or alcohol may also determine symptom subtype, and be associated with OCD (Santangelo *et al.* 1994).

Infections

There have recently been suggestions that some infections may also predispose an individual to TS. These include a special type of bacteria (streptococcus) which can cause throat infections and rheumatic fever, and the resultant recently described disorder is called PANDAS (paediatric autoimmune neuropsychiatric disorder associated with group A beta-heamolytic streptococcal infection) (Swedo *et al.* 1998). Certain viruses and Lyme disease have also produced disorders with TS symptoms. These findings, however, must be considered as speculative at this juncture (Robertson 2000).

Chapter 2

Clinical Characteristics of Tourette Syndrome

> TS has been my constant companion for decades, for as long as I can remember. Its internal rhythm of protean sensations and demands for action has always pounded away right alongside my natural cycles of thought, imagination, and concentration. (Hollenbeck 1999)

TS is now recognised to be a chronic neuropsychiatric disorder with a suggested genetic basis. Abnormalities in specific parts of the brain have also been demonstrated. In earlier years it was thought that TS was a psychological disorder, but recently there have been many studies suggesting a biological aetiology.

In today's medical and scientific worlds, there are well documented and helpful criteria according to which disorders and illnesses are classified. The two currently accepted major diagnostic systems include the *International Classification of Diseases* (10th edition) of the World Health Organisation (WHO), published in 1992, and The *Diagnostic and Statistical Manual* (DSM), (4th Edition) of the American Psychiatric Association (APA), published in 1994; previously there had been the third (1980) and third-revised (1987) editions (APA). The major differences between the two diagnostic systems are that the DSM has always had an age stipulation, by which time the symptoms must have started (but each DSM has had a different upper age limit), and the current DSM suggests that distress and significant impairment must occur, with which many authorities disagree. Both of these systems, however, include broadly the following diagnostic criteria for TS:

- multiple motor tics
- one or more vocal/phonic tics
- duration of more than one year
- age at onset below 21 years
- tics characteristically change over time
- waxing and waning of symptoms.

TS is characterised by both multiple motor tics (twitches) *and* one or more phonic (vocal) tics (noises), which occur many times a day in bouts, the number, frequency and complexity of which change over time, and they must be present for over 12 months.

The main characteristics of TS appear to be independent of culture. The symptoms, tics and noises, seem very similar, irrespective of the

Diagnostic criteria and clinical characteristics of Tourette Syndrome

country of origin. They are also suppressible (which means that the child can control them for a while at the expense of an uncomfortable inner tension). This may well lead to teachers thinking 'If Jonathan can stop his tics, then he must be putting them on – on purpose, in fact'. This is certainly not so. Tics are not only not done on purpose, but very often the child does not realise that he is doing them at all. The tics are also suggestible (which means that if a tic is mentioned, the child may well perform the tic without even thinking about it). The tics characteristically increase with stress, and decrease with distraction and concentration. They also wax and wane, which means that they occur in bouts, indicating that at some times the tics are more obvious, and at others they are less obvious, irrespective of the presence of external stimuli.

The age at onset of TS symptoms ranges from two to 21 years, with a mean of five to seven years being commonly reported, usually beginning with facial tics such as excessive eye blinking, eye rolling or nose twitching. The onset of vocal tics is usually later, with a mean age at onset of 11 years being common. The most common vocal tics are excessive sniffing and throat clearing. A recent study has shown a more favourable prognosis of TS than was previously recognised. After the onset of the tics (the average age at onset being five years), a period followed during which there is a progressive pattern of tic worsening, and the average age of the most severe tics was 10 years. By the age of 18 years, however, nearly half of the TS adolescents examined in the study were virtually tic free (Leckman *et al.* 1998). This answers one of the most common questions we get asked in the clinic: whether the child's symptoms will get worse, and whether or not the youngster will deteriorate intellectually. Fortunately, in the majority of cases we can reassure the parents that the outcome is often good.

The range of characteristic symptoms of TS is:

- premonitory sensations
- coprolalia
- copropraxia
- echolalia
- echopraxia
- palilalia
- palipraxia
- non-obscene socially inappropriate behaviours (NOSI)
- sleep difficulties.

Premonitory sensations, which many children with TS experience, are essentially different from the tics, and characteristically occur before the tics. They occur in over 80 per cent of TS patients (Cohen and Leckman 1992; Leckman *et al.* 1993), and have been very well described by Bliss (1980), a TS sufferer. These premonitary sensations have been likened to the feeling one experiences just before a sneeze, and are said by our patients to feel like an itch, a tingling sensation or, even just a generalised discomfort. These sensations often occur in the immediate location of the tic, or alternatively, can be more generally and widely distributed. We have one youngster who gets a widespread general discomfort over his abdomen, chest and neck, and the only way for him to counteract it is for him to punch himself in the neck. This is obviously distressing and painful for him to do, but also for others such as mother, teachers and us, to watch.

Coprolalia (also known as the 'swearing tic' or the 'F-word tic' and which is the inappropriate and involuntary uttering of obscenities or blasphemous words or phrases), occurs in about 10 to 30 per cent of TS patients, but in very few children or mild cases. It usually manifests itself by 15 years of age. Many patients with coprolalia try to disguise it by, for example, loud coughing and/or throat clearing, by putting their hands in front of their mouths, or by shouting or saying something else such as 'fu', 'fake', 'foot' or 'fick' instead. But in many cases the individual is unable to mask the symptom and it is then one of the most, if not the most, distressing and disabling symptoms of TS.

Children who have coprolalia often, as can be understood, get into trouble at school, since swearing in the classroom is not tolerated. Interestingly, coprolalia was recognised as early as 1885 to be part of TS, when originally described (Gilles de la Tourette 1885). 'Pure' or 'normal' swearing (which is very common today in some cultures, even amongst children, including the UK and USA) is often contextually or affectively appropriate. For example, when two young boys are arguing in the play-ground, one of them might tell the other to 'f. . . off', not be embarrassed, stick two fingers up at him, and hope that his friend leaves soon. At one level, the behaviour is not an uncommon outburst, and some may claim is congruous to the situation, and is his conscious choice. This is in sharp contrast to someone with TS who, when meeting someone for the first time, says: 'Oh hello Mr Smith, how nice to f. . . fick feet meet greet you'. This is affectively and contextually inappropriate and the perpetrator is likely to be very embarrassed and try to disguise the symptom. Some children do not even realise that they have used a swear word and are embarrassed when they are told about it, particularly if they have been brought up not to swear at all, especially in company. Sometimes coprolalia can have very adverse effects on our patients. A female patient came to the clinic recently by bus, made a loud coprolalic statement and fellow passengers called the conducter, who in turn summoned the police and had our patient removed from the bus! By the time she arrived at the clinic she was, needless to say, extremely distressed.

Copropraxia (the involuntary and inappropriate use of obscene gestures such as the V or middle finger signs) also occurs, but is thankfully not very common, occurring in some 20 per cent of clinic patients. Quite often coprolalia and copropraxia occur in the same individual, and this can produce very difficult situations. The child with TS may also disguise or hide the copropraxia, such as making the gesture under a table or desk, or putting their offending hand behind their back or behind the other hand, so that it cannot be observed by teachers or fellow pupils. Mark is an eight-year-old boy who makes the V sign from the car as his family drives along. He can't help it and would never do this on purpose, regrets it, and his mother is trying to teach him to put his entire hand up instead if he feels the need to do the tic.

Other symptoms include echolalia (the imitation of sounds or words of other people), echopraxia (the imitation of actions of other people) and palilalia (the repetition of the last word, phrase, or last syllable of a word uttered by the individual themselves). We have a patient who had to travel by train from afar to see us at the clinic. She had to put on her alarm clock in the early morning to wake her up in time. She developed echolalia (initially copying the sounds from the alarm clock), and then palilalia (repeating herself) from her clock's ticks, with the result that by the time of the hospital appointment in the afternoon, she was still saying 'Hello how are you, tick tock, tick tick, tock tock' repeatedly.

Coprolalia, echolalia and palilalia are all complex vocal tics, whereas copropraxia and echopraxia are complex motor tics. Once again, the pupil might get into trouble for expressing the symptoms of echolalia and echopraxia. If the youngster copies another child's or the teacher's movements, habits or tics, it may be felt that he is doing it on purpose: 'taking the mickey' so to speak. This may get the child into trouble, when, in fact, he is expressing involuntary symptoms of TS and cannot suppress them.

Non-obscene complex socially inappropriate behaviours (NOSI) which are also called 'disinhibition behaviours' have also been described in TS individuals. These behaviours include making aspersions about weight, height, intelligence, general appearance, breath or body odour, parts of the anatomy, and racial or ethnic slurs. NOSI is usually directed at a family member or familiar persons. Social difficulties such as verbal arguments, school problems, fist-fights, removal from a public place and legal trouble or arrest occur in about a third of patients. NOSI is more common in young boys, and is closely related to attention deficit hyperactivity disorder (ADHD) and conduct disorder (Kurlan *et al.* 1996) (see p. 13).

One of the patients who stimulated the study of NOSI by Kurlan and colleagues, lived in the area where a murder had been committed. The police were doing house to house visits to glean as much about the event that they could from people in the neighbourhood. When they visited the TS patient's home, he immediately (and falsely) admitted to having committed the crime which resulted in lengthy legal proceedings. This NOSI is also beautifully described in a novel, *Motherless Brooklyn* (Lethem 2000) in which the main and very attractive character, Lionel, has TS. Lionel is in the company of a detective after his friend has been killed. When the detective asks him his name, he replies 'Lionel Arrestme'.

Some of the symptoms (such as coprolalia, copropraxia, echolalia, echopraxia and NOSI) can be very disabling and embarrassing. It is hardly surprising, therefore, that some individuals with TS who have written books, refer to TS as an internal 'demon' which persecutes and plagues them almost constantly (Shimberg 1995; Fowler 1996).

We should like to emphasise again that:

- the majority of children with TS have it in a mild form;
- they are probably undiagnosed;
- they are not under the care of a doctor.

In one family study of TS adults and children in the community, the majority were mildly affected, and only eight out of 50 (16 per cent) individuals with TS had ever seen a doctor for symptoms (such as excessive coughing), which could be seen as part of TS (Robertson and Gourdie 1990).

Sleep difficulties occur commonly in children with TS. The abnormalities which occur include insomnia (difficulty in falling asleep, waking in the night and waking very early in the morning), sleep-talking, nightmares, night-terrors, somnambulism (sleep-walking), enuresis (urinating/wetting the bed), bruxism (grinding of the teeth), general restlessness and inability to take afternoon naps. If the child with TS has many sleep problems he may be excessively tired during the day, which may well affect his ability to concentrate and perform at school.

The traditionally held view is that TS usually has a life-long course. Commonly, the course of TS is characterised by the appearance of new tics and the disappearance of older tics (Robertson 2000). A recent study, however, has suggested a more favourable prognosis. At around the age of ten years the tics may well be at their worst and during adolesence they also tend to be more unpredictable from day to day. It was also shown that in about half of the patients the tic symptoms will remit completely by late adolesence (Leckman *et al.* 1998).

Course and prognosis

There are many reasons why pupils with TS may experience trouble with their education. Most children with TS have a normal IQ, but others experience educational problems including the effects of the tics themselves, specific learning disabilities (such as impaired visuomotor integration and deficits in executive functioning), emotional problems, reduced self-esteem and maybe even the adverse side effects of medication. Attention hyperactivity disorders (ADHD), obsessive-compulsive behaviours (OCB), anxiety and depression also may lead to further learning difficulties, and each of these will be discussed briefly and separately later.

Most studies investigating intellect in people with TS have reported the intelligence to be within the normal range. TS has, however, also been reported in learning disabled (LD) people (Golden and Greenhill 1981). Looking at the problem from a different standpoint, LD was reported in 10 per cent of one TS cohort (Golden and Hood 1982). Learning problems seem to be fairly common in people with TS. For example, Erenberg *et al.* (1986) reported learning problems in 36 per cent of 200 children with TS.

Intellectual abilities, learning problems, cognitive abilities or impairment

A classic paper by Golden in 1984 reviewed 13 studies and put forward some suggestions as to the neuropsychological abnormalities in TS. He suggested that there was evidence of 'organic dysfunction' in many patients tested, as evidenced by the fact that there was a difference between VIQ (verbal IQ) and PIQ (performance IQ) of more than 15 points. Language skills in TS subjects appear to be largely unimpaired. Memory impairment does not appear to be a problem in individuals with TS, although one study found impairment of immediate recall of a verbally presented story (Sutherland *et al.* 1982). In the studies reviewed, arithmetic skills appeared to be below those in reading and spelling words.

By and large it seems that medication has no consistent effects on the IQ of people with TS (Golden 1984; Schultz *et al.* 1999). In an early study from our group, however, 90 patients with TS were studied using the Wechsler Intelligence Scales (WAIS for adults, WISC for children). Results indicated that patients who had never had medication (neuroleptics, see p. 33) at all had significantly higher Full, Performance and Verbal IQs. Using a special self-report scale in the adult TS patients (the Mood Adjective Checklist, which differentiates between depression and fatigue), patients on medication rated themselves as more fatigued, but not as more depressed than those not taking medication (Robertson *et al.* 1988). In another study from our group, however, none of the correlations between performance on the experimental tasks and use of medication (such as neuroleptics or SSRIs – see pp. 33–9), reached significance (Channon *et al.* 1992).

There have been several controlled studies conducted mostly on children with TS which have suggested that visuomotor integration (VMI) appears to be one of the main areas of functioning which is most impaired in TS (Schultz *et al.* 1999). In practice, what does this mean? It indicates that the pupil with TS may not be able accurately to copy both simple and/or complex geometric designs and figures when asked to do so. This obviously has implications for the TS pupil at school. The child with TS may not be able to complete some tasks where copying a design is necessary either from the blackboard or from a book, and thus he may fall behind in that particular lesson or subject.

Another main problem area for children with TS has been suggested to be that of 'executive functioning'. This refers to a broad range of functions including forward planning, cognitive/mental flexibility and sustained attention. Although many studies implicate abnormal executive functioning, a review of the results of these suggests that there is inconsistency in the findings (Schultz *et al.* 1999). Thus, more studies in this area have still to be undertaken.

Other problems children with TS may encounter include the effects of the tics themselves. If a pupil has a head-turning tic, for example, he may not be able to look at the blackboard for a sustained period of time. If the child has severe tics involving the hands or arms, this may seriously interfere with writing which can obviously disadvantage the child both at school and when doing homework. We recently assessed a child with a dystonic posture (abnormally turned outwards hand) which affected his writing a great deal: he wrote both very slowly and untidily, to the point of almost being illegible.

Loud vocal tics clearly can be very disruptive in the classroom and can disturb not only the child who is making the noises but also the other pupils, especially if the child with TS makes almost continuous sniffing or throat clearing sounds. Mark had motor tics which were quite mild; however, he had an almost constant sniffing tic which drove his family and classmates to despair. They would ask him to keep quiet or even go and watch television in another room where he could not disturb them.

There is no doubt at all that stress also makes tics worse. Therefore, for example, when a child is asked to do something in front of the whole class, he may become very stressed, experience a great increase in tics, and as a result perform badly.

Many TS children have emotional problems and reduced self-esteem. This may arise out of personal embarrassment as the child realises that he is different from other pupils (such as performing strange tics), or sadly as a result of teasing and bullying, to which many of our TS children in the clinic are subject from their peers, and in a couple of cases even from teachers. We have seen children in the clinic who have been made to wear a dunce's hat and stand in shame in front of the rest of their class. The resulting reduction in self-esteem is a serious consequence for children with TS, and we consider the ethos and values in a school that demonstrably promotes equal opportunities for all and learning strategies to overcome this as paramount in the education of the child with TS.

It has also been shown that TS may be associated with a few specific behaviours or problems. These include, in particular and most commonly: attention deficit hyperactivity disorder (ADHD); obsessive-compulsive behaviours (OCB); obsessive-compulsive disorder (OCD); self-injurious behaviours (SIB).

Conditions commonly associated with Tourette Syndrome

Attention deficit hyperactivity disorder (ADHD)

ADHD is defined as a persistent pattern of inattention and/or hyperactivity-impulsivity that is more frequent and severe than is typically encountered in individuals at a comparable level of development. Some symptoms must have been present before the age of seven years, they must cause significant impairment and interference with functioning, and symptoms must be present in two or more settings. It is more common in boys, and is often associated with antisocial behaviours and conduct disorder. Causative factors may include genetic factors, poverty, alcohol abuse in the parents, dietary factors (such as lead ingestion/absorption) and exposure to tranquillisers.

It is worth noting that ADHD is the disorder in the DSM (APA) classification, whereas hyperkinetic disorder is the ICD (WHO) classification (Overmeyer and Taylor 1999). In this book, ADHD will be used.

It has been stated that the differences between countries in the prevalence of ADHD and hyperkinetic disorder have generated controversy, and a large part of the difference is due to differences in definition rather than from geographical differences. Using the DSM definition, ADHD is found in five to 10 per cent of the population (5 per cent in the UK), and using the ICD definition hyperkinetic disorder in one to two per cent of the population (2 per cent in the UK) (Swanson *et al.* 1998).

Children with ADHD are at a significantly greater risk for many psychological and social problems including developmental delays, poor academic performance, school behaviour problems, poor peer social skills and increased conflict in parent–child and teacher–child interactions (Barkley *et al.* 2000).

In the classroom, pupils with TS and ADHD may show signs of inattention and poor concentration, and therefore have messy, sloppy, incomplete and careless work which they hand in late, if at all. They often appear to be daydreaming, not listening to the teacher and are very distractable. They may start one task and not finish it, yet go on to another task, and they may fail to complete their schoolwork.

Signs of hyperactivity include:

- excessive fidgetiness
- squirming
- not remaining seated in the classroom
- excessive running about or climbing in the classroom
- having difficulties in playing quietly
- appearing constantly 'on the go'
- talking excessively.

Impulsivity is recognised by impatience, blurting out answers before the questions have been completed by the teachers, having difficulty in awaiting turns, and frequently interrupting the other children. Other symptoms of ADHD include having difficulty in converting words into concepts, having difficulty in following instructions, deviating from what the class is supposed to be doing, calling out of turn, exhibiting aggressive behaviours towards classmates, losing and forgetting equipment and lacking social skills (Cooper and Ideus 1996).

ADHD is one of the most common psychiatric disorders affecting children, with prevalence estimates ranging from around two per cent in the UK, to eight per cent in the USA (Swanson *et al.* 1998), whereas in children with TS seen in clinics, ADHD occurs in between 20 to 90 per cent (Robertson and Eapen 1992), clearly well in excess of the prevalence in the general population. Of importance, however, is that even two epidemiological studies in the community have shown high rates of ADHD in individuals with TS. The rate of ADHD in young adults in Israel with TS was eight per cent (Apter *et al.* 1993), compared with a population prevalence of around four per cent. In a school study in the UK four out of five pupils with probable or definite TS were reported as hyperactive; one satisfied diagnostic criteria for ADHD (Mason *et al.* 1998). Although the numbers in the latter study were small (five children identified as having TS or probable TS out of 166 school children studied), we feel it is important to highlight it, as it is one of the few studies which has adressed this issue of ADHD in TS in a non-clinic population.

The precise relationship between ADHD and TS is complex and has recently been reviewed by Robertson (2000). There appear to be several possibilities as to the nature of the relationship between TS and ADHD. There have been suggestions that the two disorders are always genetically related, or that ADHD may be secondary to TS and genetically related only in a sub-group of TS subjects. On the other hand, children with TS may have reduced capacities for concentration, attention and impulse control, but at a level subthreshold for a diagnosis of ADHD (Robertson 2000). It has recently been shown that children with TS and ADHD have more behaviour problems and poorer social adaptation than children with TS alone, or children without either diagnosis (Carter *et al.* 2000).

Frequently children with TS only are impulsive and loud and thus if they also have ADHD may well need significant levels of support in home and at school to teach them how to cope adequately with their symptoms. These children may be extremely impulsive, overactive and loud, and be difficult to manage either in the classroom or on the playground.

Obsessive-compulsive disorder (OCD) and obsessive-compulsive behaviours (OCB)

Pure or primary obsessive-compulsive disorder (OCD) is characterised by persistent obsessions (which are recurrent, intrusive, senseless thoughts) or compulsions (repetitive and purposeful behaviours, which are performed according to certain rules or in a stereotyped fashion); they must be a significant source of distress to the individual and/or interfere with the individual's functioning and exceed one hour per day. Many of the obsessions and compulsions in OCD concern germs, dirt and contamination. For example, the person has thoughts of being dirty and therefore has to wash excessively and unnecessarily. It is suggested that OCD is somewhat rare in childhood with a prevalence of about 0.3 per cent, although it has been pointed out that isolated compulsions, such as not walking on certain paving stones, are common.

Reports have shown that 11 to 80 per cent of patients with TS have obsessive-compulsive behaviours (OCB). Many subsequent investigations, however, have shown differences between primary OCD and the OCB encountered in TS. In essence, the obsessions seen in TS have to do with sexual, violent, religious, aggressive and symmetrical themes; the compulsions are to do with checking, ordering, counting, repeating, forced touching and a concern with symmetry (for reviews see Robertson 1989; 1995; 2000). There is also general agreement that at least some forms of OCB are genetically related to TS (Pauls *et al.* 1986; Eapen *et al.* 1993).

Several studies have also documented significant obsessive-compulsive symptomatology (OCS) in children with TS. For example, Leonard *et al.* (1992) studied 54 children who participated in a treatment study of OCD and in which TS had been an exclusionary criterion, two to seven years later. At follow-up eight boys met diagnostic criteria for TS; except for their earlier age at onset of OCD, the patients with TS were indistinguishable from the OCD group.

De Groot *et al.* (1995) examined 92 children and adolescents with TS through self-measure and parents' assessment of a variety of characteristics including OCS in a postal questionnaire survey. None of the participants had been referred for clinical evaluation. There was a significant positive relationship between tic severity and OCS. Obsessions contributed to the prediction of learning problems, perfectionism, and antisocial behaviour; compulsions contributed to the prediction of hyperactivity, psychosomatic symptoms, perfectionism and muscular tension.

In our clinic many of the children with TS are highly obsessional with a wide variety of these obsessional thoughts and compulsive behaviours. In a cohort of 90 adults and children with TS, 33 (about 30 per cent) were obsessional (Robertson *et al.* 1988).

Pupils with TS who also have OCB/OCD may be perfectionists, try to get their work done 'just right' and therefore go over and over things until they feel comfortable with the result, which may not be at all obvious to an outside observer such as the parent or teacher. They may spend an enormous amount of time tidying their desk, so much so that they do not get their work done. They may have obsessions (repetitive intrusive thoughts) which prevent them from concentrating on their work. We treat many children in the clinic who are very distressed by their obsessions and compulsions. A little boy we saw recently cried every time his distressing obsessions were mentioned by others, such as ourselves in the clinic. Fairly often even in children with mild TS, but with severe OCB/OCD (such as the little boy just described), we find that it is appropriate for us to offer treatment for these particular symptoms.

Self-injurious behaviours (SIB)

Self-injurious behaviours are also seen in children with TS, and SIB is often related to obsessionality. These SIB can include, for instance, pulling one's hair out resulting in bald patches (trichotillomania), head banging, hurting one's eyes, punching and slapping oneself and/or hurting oneself with hard objects such as school pencils. SIB has also been shown to be related to TS severity (Robertson *et al.* 1989).

Rage

Recently it has been suggested that rage is an important symptom in children and adolescents with TS (Budman *et al.* 1998). Precisely how common rage is in the context of TS is difficult to establish, as few studies have enquired about it specifically. This rage seems to be associated with OCD and ADHD and in some subjects with oppositional defiant disorder and conduct disorder (see p. 22).

It has been recently suggested (Robertson and Baron-Cohen 1998) that it may be useful to subdivide TS clinically into three types:

1. **Pure TS**, which consists primarily and almost solely of motor tics (or twitches) and phonic (vocal) tics or noises.
2. **Full blown TS**, which includes coprophenomena, echophenomena, and paliphenomena.
3. **TS-Plus**, in which an individual also has ADHD, significant OCB or OCD, and SIB. Others with severe psychopathology (such as depression, anxiety, personality disorder) and other difficult behaviours (oppositional defiant disorder, conduct disorder and some learning problems) may also be included in this group.

It is suspected that, with few exceptions, children with TS who are identified in the community such as in school studies, and who are unknown to medical services, will be mostly of the first type, whereas children referred to the clinic fall into the latter two categories. In the recent study referred to earlier embracing 3,500 TS clinic patients, only 12 per cent had pure TS with no comorbidity at all (Freeman *et al.* 2000).

Types of Tourette Syndrome

There are several instruments used to assess various aspects of TS, such as the National Hospital Interview Schedule; the Diagnostic Confidence Index; the Yale Global Tic Severity Scale; the MOVES Scale for Tourette's Syndrome; the Hopkins Motor and Vocal Tic Severity Scale; the TS Videotaped Scale; and the Tourette Syndrome Severity Scale. These are discussed more fully below.

Diagnostic and assessment tools for use in Tourette Syndrome

The National Hospital Interview Schedule (NHIS)

The National Hospital Interview Schedule for the assessment of Gilles de la Tourette syndrome (Robertson and Eapen 1996) is a clinician rated assessment schedule and semi-structured interview which allows a standardised diagnosis of TS to be made. It contains sections for personal and family history, associated symptoms (such as coprophenomena, echophenomena, palilalia, OCB, SIB etc.) and it also has a section in which the clinician notes which tics he or she has seen or heard at interview. Both history and examination are important, but in order for a diagnosis to be made, tics must be observed by the clinician as well as being obtained on history taking. The interview takes between two and three hours depending on the complexity of the patient and the experience of the clinician.

The Diagnostic Confidence Index (DCI)

The Diagnostic Confidence Index (Robertson *et al.* 1999) is a clinician rated instrument which was developed by the clinical members of the American Tourette Syndrome Association International Genetic Consortium. The DCI uses a lifetime history and examination, and thus allows an assessment of the lifetime likelihood of an individual having TS. The DCI produces a score from 0 to 100 and consists of a list of 26 weighted 'confidence factors', the sum of which gives the score, the mean of which in one large study of nearly 300 diagnosed patients with TS was 61 per cent.

The Yale Global Tic Severity Scale (YGTSS)

The Yale Global Tic Severity Scale (Leckman *et al.* 1989) is a clinician rated semi-structured interview used to assess TS severity. The scale takes into account symptoms present during the previous week. For both motor and vocal tics, the clinician rates the number, frequency, intensity, complexity and interference (of functioning by the tics), as well as a global rating of overall impairment. The scores range from 0 to 100 per cent. The YGTSS can be used during treatment to assess whether or not the patient is responding to medication.

The MOVES Scale for Tourette's Syndrome

The Motor tic, Obsessions and compulsions, Vocal tic Evaluation Survey (MOVES) (Gaffney *et al.* 1994) is a self-report scale for many symptoms of TS and was designed to be quickly and easily completed by children, adolescents or adults. It generates scores on five sub-scales and it has been demonstrated that individuals with TS score higher than other people who do not have TS. It takes one to five minutes to complete. It correlates well with the YGTSS and is sensitive to change.

The Hopkins Motor and Vocal Tic Severity Scale (Hopkins Scale)

The Hopkins Motor and Vocal Tic Severity Scale (Walkup *et al.* 1992) is an instrument which combines self-report (usually parent) information together with a clinician's assessment, and these are combined to form a total score. The scale essentially consists of a series of linear analogue scales with a score of 1 to 5 for each. The list of symptoms is individualised and modified in an on-going fashion to reflect the patient's current tics, and takes into account tics during the previous week.

The TS Videotaped Scale

In the TS Videotaped Scale (Goetz *et al.* (1987), patients are videotaped in three settings: sitting quietly with the examiner in the room, reading aloud with the examiner in the room and sitting quietly without the examiner in the room. The examiner then reviews the tapes and assesses both motor and vocal tic severity. Five tic variables are measured including number of body areas affected, frequency of motor and vocal tics, and severity of motor and vocal tics.

The Tourette Syndrome Severity Scale (TSSS)

The Tourette Syndrome Severity Scale (Shapiro *et al.* 1983; 1988) is completed by the clinician and provides a measure of severity of tic symptoms. Parents and significant others assist the doctor to rate the degree to which the tics:

- are noticeable to others
- elicit comments or curiosity
- interfere with functioning whether or not the patient is incapacitated, homebound or hospitalised, and/or
- cause the child with TS to appear odd or bizarre.

In our clinic we routinely use the NHIS, the DCI, the YGTSS, the MOVES and, in research protocols, we may use the Goetz *et al.* video instrument as well. This facilitates an accurate as possible assessment of the phenomenology of the TS as well as a measure of its severity.

Chapter 3

Co-morbid Conditions

TS has been conceptualised as a psychological problem, a neurological problem, and more recently a neurobehavioural problem. (Walkup 1999)

Despite the fact it is acknowledged that many children with TS have behaviour disturbances, there are very few prospective studies reporting the psychiatric aspects of children with TS. In the studies which have been conducted, and certainly in our own clinical experience, the conditions which can be encountered in children include depression, anxiety, oppositional defiant disorder and conduct disorder, which are discussed more fully below.

There is debate however as to whether or not these conditions are truly increased in children with TS or whether they reflect referral bias (Berkson 1946). Essentially this means that children seen in hospital clinics may well *not* be representative of all children with TS, such as those with a mild TS who are not being treated by a doctor and who are unknown to health professionals.

Depression

Depression is a well recognised medical disorder. It is included as a major disorder and its features are characteristic. Recent research indicates a prevalence for depression in about one per cent of prepubertal children.

Common symptoms of depressive illness include depressed sad hopeless mood, loss of interest or pleasure, altered appetite, disturbed sleep (inability in getting off to sleep, waking in the middle of the night and feeling internally uncomfortable, or waking early in the morning and being unable to go to sleep again), feeling worse in the morning, agitation or restlessness, retardation or being slowed up, decreased energy, sense of worthlessness or guilt, poor concentration, low self-esteem and thoughts of death or suicide.

Depression has been studied in patients with TS, but most studies have examined depressive symptomatology rather than depressive illness. In general it appears that depression is more common in people (children included) with TS than in the general population.

Thus, in our studies, depression (as measured by the well known Beck Depression Inventory, a self-rating scale used to measure depression) has been shown to be common in adults with TS (Robertson *et al.* 1988), and the depression scores to be significantly higher in adults with TS when compared to healthy adult controls who do not have TS (Robertson *et al.* 1993; 1997).

To the best of our knowledge only two published studies have specifically examined depression in children with TS. Ferrari *et al.* (1984) studied 10 TS children. Their parents reported high levels of depression in the children, but no measures of the child's depression (neither self-rated nor examined) was used. Wodrich *et al.* (1997) used the Personality Inventory for Children to study 33 children with TS, which is completed by parents rather than by the children themselves. Results indicated that the TS children, when compared to 66 healthy 'control' children were rated as having a high rate of psychiatric disorders, especially depression, which was found in 73 per cent.

In addition, in our clinic many of the children have substantial depressive symptomatology which, in some cases, qualifies for depressive illness, which in turn requires appropriate treatment.

Ironically, some of the medications such as haloperidol, sulpiride and clonidine used in the treatment of TS can have a side effect of depressed mood.

If the teacher notices that a child with tics or TS looks or acts depressed, he or she should inform the head teacher or a member of the school's Senior Management Team (SMT) and discuss what steps should, if necessary, be taken to consult with the pupil, parent or other agencies.

Anxiety

There are many types of anxiety disorders, but some of the main ones include panic attacks, agorophobia, specific phobias, social phobias and generalised anxiety disorder (GAD). GAD is characterised by persistent and excessive anxiety and worry (APA 1994). GAD is the most common emotional disorder in childhood and is characterised by both physical components (such as palpitations – heart beating fast and loud – or a dry mouth) and psychological components (such as fear); abdominal pain is also common. Predisposing factors include the child's own temperament and parental overprotection.

There has always been an understanding that TS children are anxious, but the area has not really been studied in great depth. Robertson (2000) reviewed 8 studies in the USA and one in Australia examining anxiety in TS individuals (both adults and children). In general, anxiety was encountered in between 30 and 44 per cent of TS patients, and specific diagnoses included 'severe anxiety', GAD, panic disorder, separation anxiety disorder and phobias. In several studies, TS patients had significantly more anxiety than did healthy 'normal' control individuals without an illness.

In our clinic we have examined anxiety in several settings. In all studies we have demonstrated that TS patients have more anxiety than the normative data and also than healthy controls (Robertson *et al*. 1988; 1993; 1997). In our clinic, although not studied formally, many of the TS youngsters are anxious and of course when they have bad tics, they become more anxious.

The side effects of certain medications used in the treatment of TS can also cause anxiety and mimic both school phobia and separation anxiety, both of which are common types of anxiety in children.

It thus does seem that individuals with TS, including youngsters, are more anxious than their healthy counterparts and significant proportions of TS clinic populations have symptoms of anxiety and many even qualify for having an anxiety disorder.

Anxious pupils with TS may be hypervigilant, obviously worry excessively that something is going to happen to them, worry that their work is not good enough, and they may also look anxious. Children with TS may also be worried that their tics and other symptoms may be observed by the teacher and other children in the class which, in turn, makes them even more anxious and tic more.

Oppositional defiant disorder (ODD) and conduct disorder (CD)

The characteristic features of oppositional defiant disorder (ODD) include recurring patterns of negativistic, defiant, disobedient and hostile behaviours towards authority figures that persist for at least six months. These behaviours include the child frequently losing his/her temper, consistently arguing with adults, actively defying or refusing to comply with requests or rules of adults, deliberately doing things that will annoy other people, blaming others for their own behaviours, being easily touchy or annoyed by others, being angry or resentful and finally being spiteful and vindictive. In order to qualify for the diagnosis, the behaviours must be more evident than of those peers who do not have this disorder, and must have led to significant impairment in functioning. Other disorders such as ADHD, learning disorders and communication disorders are also commonly associated with ODD. Boys are more commonly affected and rates of ODD of two to 15 per cent have been reported.

Conduct disorder (CD) is characterised by a repetitive pattern of behaviour in which the basic rights of others or major age-appropriate societal norms or rules are violated. The behaviours fall into four main groups:

- aggressive conduct that causes or threatens physical harm to other people or animals;
- non-aggressive conduct that results in property loss or damage (e.g. fire setting);
- deceitfulness or theft;
- serious violations of rules.

Children with CD may start fights, may show bullying, threatening or intimidating behaviours, may use a weapon, and can be physically cruel to people or animals, lie, steal and/or force an individual into sexual activity, stay out at night or run away from home. Youngsters with CD may abuse substances (smoke tobacco, drink alcohol, abuse drugs) and engage in risky and reckless acts. Aetiological (causal) factors include both genetics and environment, boys are more commonly affected, the prevalence in general population children is about four per cent, and low self-esteem and poor peer relationships are present in about 20 per cent of youngsters with CD. CD is considered a behavioural disorder rather than an emotional disorder, and the term 'delinquency' refers to the subgroup of children or youngsters who break the law.

There has always been some debate as to whether or not children with TS have significant problems with ODD and CD. Not many controlled studies exist, and few have employed DSM/ICD criteria. Mason *et al.* (1998) examined pupils with tics in a west Essex school, and teachers rated them as having significantly more CD or emotional disorders. Freeman *et al.* (2000) documented that substantial proportions of 3,500 clinic patients with TS had behavioural problems with males having more than females with regards to CD/ODD (16 per cent for males, 11 per cent for females) and anger control problems (38 per cent for males, 30 per cent for females).

In our specialist clinic there is no doubt that many of the children with TS who are assessed have either ODD or CD or both. Most of these children also have ADHD. We have, however, not yet performed a controlled analysis and so, are not currently able to say whether the TS children have more of these disturbances than do their peers who do not have these disorders.

Chapter 4
Differential Diagnosis

Psychiatric diagnosis is an uncertain art. . . [during which] clinicians and researchers have evolved a common language that is based on behaviors, observable features, and the reports patients have offered about distressing mental experiences. (Towbin *et al.* 1999)

What can Tourette Syndrome be mistaken for?

There are many disorders which can be similar to TS and they need to be considered in what doctors call the 'differential diagnosis'. Disorders which are in the differential diagnosis include: transient tic disorder; chronic multiple tic disorder; allergy; chorea; Sydenham's chorea; Huntington's Disease; Wilson's Disease; dystonia; tardive Tourettism; epilepsy; phenylketonuria; autistic spectrum disorders; psychoactive substance abuse. Of these, the most common differential diagnoses by far will be transient tic disorder and chronic multiple tic disorder.

Transient tic disorder

Transient tic disorder (TTD) is diagnosed when there are single or multiple motor and/or vocal tics which occur for at least four weeks, but not for longer than 12 consecutive months. The onset of the tics must be before the age of 18 years (APA 1994).

Chronic multiple tic disorder

Chronic motor or vocal tic disorder (CMT or CVT) is diagnosed when there are single or multiple motor or vocal tics, but not both, which occur for longer than 12 consecutive months. The onset of the tics must be before the age of 18 years (APA 1994).

Allergy

Many of the symptoms of TS are also common in people who suffer from allergies; these symptoms include sniffing, throat clearing, nose twitching and eye blinking. Many of these children with TS are therefore referred first to an allergist (Shimberg 1995). There are however few studies formally examining allergy in people with TS. Bruun (1984) reviewed her experience with over 300 patients with TS. She stated that although there is no evidence that allergy is causative of TS, many of her patients had an increase in symptoms of TS associated with seasonal allergy responses. Although some have reported exacerbation of TS symptoms on exposure to allergens (Rapp 1986; Mandell 1986), there is no scientific evidence for the involvement of allergy in TS (Finegold 1985). In a study we undertook (Robertson, Kalali, Brostoff – unpublished data), there was no increase in allergy in clinic patients with TS when compared to patients from general practices.

Chorea

Chorea, derived from the Latin word to dance, refers to irregularly timed (arrhythmic), random, brief purposeless involuntary movements which can be generalised or confined to certain parts of the body (such as arms and hands), which may give the appearance of restlessness. If it occurs in the facial area, a variety of facial expressions and tongue protusion may occur. It is important to note that chorea may occur as a normal part of infant development within the first three months of life. There are several kinds of hereditary choreas including benign familial chorea, which is dominantly inherited and begins in the first decade and is usually non-progressive (Trinidad and Kurlan 1995).

Sydenham's chorea

Sydenham's chorea or St Vitus's Dance is a movement disorder which occurs more frequently in female children and in about three-quarter of cases is associated with streptococcal pharyngitis (sore red throat) or rheumatic fever. The onset is usually between the ages of five and 15 years. The streptococcal infection usually precedes the movements by one to six months. The chorea worsens over two to four weeks, persists for a while, and then resolves over three to six months. Changes in behaviour are also common and include for example, OCB (Trinidad and Kurlan 1995).

Huntington's disease

Huntington's disease (HD, Huntington's chorea) is a degenerative movement disorder which usually begins between the ages of 30 and 50 years, but it may occur in childhood as early as the age of four in the juvenile form. Approximately 10 per cent of HD gene carriers have the juvenile onset form (signs of illness before the age of 20 years), called the Westphal variant. In the majority of the childhood onset cases, inheritance is from the father. HD is often associated with behavioural/emotional changes (such as depression) and difficulties, and nearly always with dementia (substantial cognitive decline). It affects the genders equally. It is a genetic disorder transmitted by a single autosomal dominant gene located on chromosome four (Trinidad and Kurlan 1995).

Wilson's disease

Wilson's disease (WD) or hepato-lenticular degeneration usually begins between the ages of 10 and 25 years. It is a movement disorder associated with depositions of copper in the eyes (Kayser Fleischer rings), liver and certain parts of the brain, as well as abnormal amounts of copper in the blood and urine. The point has been made that no two patients with WD are exactly the same. Younger patients with WD can have movement disorders including dystonia, tremor, choreiform (writhing) movements, dysarthria (difficulty with speaking) and drooling, clumsiness with the hands, a change of personality and intellectual deterioration. Often there is also a deterioration in the performance at school, attributed to laziness. Eye, blood and urine tests can confirm the diagnosis. WD is a genetic disorder with an abnormal gene on chromosome 13 (Walshe 1995).

Dystonia

Dystonia is essentially stiffening and twisting of certain muscle groups, resulting in abnormal sustained postures. This can include the well known conditions of writer's cramp and spasmodic torticollis (wry neck). If the legs are involved, the patient may well be crippled. Dystonia can be grouped according to age and two of the three groups begin under 21 years of age. There are many causes of dystonia including genetics and inborn errors of metabolism (Trinidad and Kurlan 1995), but it is also important to note that dystonic tics can occur in children with TS.

Tardive Tourettism

Neuroleptic or antipsychotic medication (see p. 33 under treatment) can be given to youngsters for behavioural problems, autism and psychotic illness. During short-term or long-term treatment with these medications, symptoms identical to TS may develop and this is called 'tardive TS' or 'Tardive Tourettism' (Robertson 2000).

Epilepsy

Some patients with epilepsy have seizures during which they have muscle movements, but they also have a classic loss or alteration of consciousness. Some patients with myoclonic epilepsy have muscle jerking associated with no loss of consciousness. Many of our patients with repetitive eye blinking or staring tics have been (incorrectly) thought to have epilepsy.

Phenylketonuria

Phenylketonuria (PKU) is an autosomal dominant disorder, with an abnormal gene on chromosome 12. PKU may be detected on routine neonatal screening, and results in cognitive impairment. Movement disorders may also occur in PKU and include stiff muscles, rigidity, tremor and chorea-athetosis (writhing movements), and treatment is by dietary restriction (Thompson 1995).

Autistic spectrum disorders with tics and stereotypes

Autism is a neurobehavioural syndrome in which there is a cluster of abnormal behaviours. These include an impairment in reciprocal social interaction, impairment in verbal and non-verbal communication and in imaginative activity and a markedly restricted repetitive and stereotyped repertoire of behaviours, activities and interests. In the World Health Organisation's (1992) criteria, the presence of abnormal/impaired development must be noted before the age of three years. Thus, the child's social relationships and developments are abnormal, the child fails to develop normal communication, and the child's interests are not flexible and imaginative as are those of many other children. Autism, as with TS, occurs more often in males, but is often associated with learning disability (Baron-Cohen and Bolton 1993). Children with autism may well have associated tics and stereotypies (movements which occur frequently and repetitively but also have a pattern to them).

Asperger's Syndrome is a condition thought to fall within the 'autistic spectrum' which is characterised by subtle impairments in social communication, social interaction and social imagination which affects individuals in the average to above average range and more commonly affects males (Cumine *et al.* 1998). Children with Asperger's Syndrome may also have tics which do not necessarily meet criteria for TS.

Psychoactive substance abuse

Iatrogenic (medically prescribed) drugs such as methylphenidate can precipitate tics in vulnerable individuals, and the chronic abuse of some recreational drugs, such as those from the amphetamine family, can produce tics and hyperactive type behaviours.

Chapter 5

Management and Treatment of Tourette Syndrome

Because the use of pharmacotherapy does not eliminate TS, lead to a cure, or alter the long-term prognosis, the decision on whether or not to use medication is based on the impact that TS has on the individual's quality of life.

(Erenberg 1999)

Before discussing the particular management of TS we would like to emphasise that all professionals involved should aim at the optimal treatment of the child as a whole, and that it is becoming increasingly accepted that if an individual has a chronic condition (such as TS), the patient must become a partner in the treatment process (Holman and Lorig 2000). It is also important to note that increasingly children are becoming service evaluators with regards to education, paediatrics and mental health (Hennessy 1999). Thus it is highly recommended that a holistic approach is adopted where the child becomes involved in treatment if at all possible; and we suggest that the treatment may well be more satisfactory where the child is asked for his/her views on the progress of and satisfaction with the treatment.

The complex management of TS has been comprehensively reviewed by Robertson (2000), while Eapen and Robertson (2000) have also made practical suggestions, especially in the medical or pharmacological treatment of TS and OCD occurring together.

When discussing the management of TS, firstly, it is imperative for the child with TS and his/her family to go to a specialist who knows about TS as only then will they be able to have expert assessment and management. Unfortunately, if the general practitioner has not heard of TS, parents and their children may initially be referred to clinicians of the wrong speciality. For example, often parents are referred with their children with excessive blinking to an eye doctor (or ophthalmologist), but after an examination are told that all is well; all with the eyes is in fact well. TS is not an eye disorder, it is a tic disorder of which one very common tic is excessive blinking. Other parents may take their children with excessive sniffing, throat clearing and coughing to a throat doctor (or ENT surgeon), but after an examiniation are told that all is well; in fact nothing is wrong with the nose and throat. TS is a generalised tic disorder of which vocal (phonic) tics include sniffing, throat clearing and coughing.

Fortunately, more and more youngsters are being correctly referred for treatment of their TS but even in the hands of an expert, the correct management of TS is complex. It can include:

- psycho-education
- psychotherapy
- behavioural treatments
- medications
- psychosurgery.

Psycho-education

Management of TS is extremely important in the clinic and includes, at one end of the spectrum, very practical information, called psycho-education, of the youngster with TS and his or her family. In our clinic we routinely do an in-depth assessment of the child and after this, make or, in some cases, confirm the diagnosis of TS. Not all children who are referred have TS.

Our initial assessment can take between two and four hours depending on many factors, including how severe the child's TS is, how complex the family dynamics are, how many associated behaviours the child has, and whether or not the child with TS is depressed or has severe ADHD.

We then inform the child and his family about TS and aspects that are especially important to the child with TS. We discuss in detail:

- the likely cause(s), such as genetics in the majority of cases
- the prognosis – highlighting the fact that in recent times, the prognosis is better than was previously thought
- the associated behaviours encountered in individuals with TS.

We also hand out a *fact sheet* about each patient (see Appendix B) which they take home with them, describing which symptoms they have (and the medical names for the symptoms) and the implications thereof.

In addition we offer *supportive reassurance* to the patient and the family and, this reassurance may be sufficient for some patients, especially for those with mild symptoms.

In our clinic we also give the patients a *reading list* which includes books written by TS sufferers (Fowler 1996, Schimberg 1995), advice about TS (Hearle 1992), the chapters in books by the well known Dr Oliver Sacks (1987; 1995), the book written for patients with TS and their families co-authored by one of us (Robertson and Baron-Cohen 1998), and, in some instances, our TS scientific publication list.

We provide the patients and their families with the 'Questions and Answers' leaflet of the Tourette Syndrome Association (UK) and give them practical information about the Association. In the UK and USA and in many other countries there are Tourette Syndrome Associations which provide written information about TS, have help lines staffed by knowledgeable individuals, organise both supportive and scientific meetings for sufferers, carers and professionals interested in TS, and, in some instances, fund research.

We also offer to, and often do, write *letters* to teachers, head teachers, or other relevant personnel in the children's schools. It goes without saying that we obtain the parents' written consent before sending the letter.

Psychological techniques and psychotherapy

Psychological therapy or psychotherapy is essentially based on the verbal communication between the patient and the therapist, and it also relies on the relationship between the two participating individuals. Psychotherapy aims to help individuals cope, adjust to life, relieve uncomfortable symptoms, facilitate their rehabilitation and allow them to lead as full a life as possible. Katona and Robertson (2000) have suggested and described the following types of psychotherapy: counselling, supportive psychotherapy, psychoanalysis, cognitive-behaviour therapy and behavioural therapies and these are more fully described below.

Counselling

Counselling is a widely used form of therapy in which certain characteristics of the therapist are crucial, and they include empathy, positivity and genuineness. There are also several types of specific interventions included under counselling, such as the provision of information, problem solving and support. In treating a child with TS counselling is thus very important and indeed we use this intervention with every patient with TS whom we see. It may well be appropriate to involve also informed school counsellors in helping the child with TS.

It is important that the child with TS feels as though he is being understood and listened to, and we reassure the child and the parents that the child is not strange or bizarre, and that there are many thousands (probably millions world-wide) of children and young persons who also have TS. We have been told in our clinic that it is of great comfort to the children and their families that we have seen literally hundreds of youngsters with TS.

For many children with TS who have mild symptoms, reassurance and support will often suffice. Particular problems may have to be solved and these may include the strategy to be developed to cope with a particular tic. Some of our children and youngsters with TS, for example, learn how to use more acceptable words instead of an unacceptable word in public. This sometimes needs professional help, but it is remarkable how many parents and youngsters work out strategies for themselves, after some initial advice from us. For example we have several children whose parents have suggested that if they realise that they are going to use a swear word, they use a nonsense word instead.

Supportive psychotherapy

Supportive psychotherapy is really the simplest form of psychotherapy and in this form of therapy the doctor or therapist assesses the patient's life situation by allowing the individual to talk freely about him or herself, their symptoms and their problems. The doctor or therapist then is able to help the patient make changes within his/her lifestyle, symptoms or anxieties, and thus become more functional. The patients may be seen for a brief time perhaps for a few weeks, or the therapy may last for several months.

For children with TS this type of therapy can prove to be very useful indeed. Individuals may express difficulties they have in coping with certain symptoms, such as embarrassing tics, or following teasing, bullying or rejection. It has been suggested that that most common indications for formal psychotherapy in youngsters with TS are low self-esteem, impairing anxiety or depression, and poor relationships with family and peers (King *et al.* 1999).

Psychoanalysis

Psychoanalysis is a form of psychotherapy and it also refers to the school of psychology founded by Sigmund Freud. It stresses, *inter alia*, the importance of childhood experience in forming the personality. The patient sees the analyst several times a week for a specified amount of time; this type of therapy can last from as long as two to five years. In our opinion, psychoanalysis would not be able to help the tics *per se*. In addition there are few child psycho-analysts who have enough knowledge of TS to enable a successful therapeutic alliance to develop.

Cognitive-behaviour therapy

Cognitive-behaviour therapy (CBT) was originally described by Aaron Beck for treating depressive illness. This type of therapy was based on observations that patients who were depressed had essentially negative thoughts about themselves, their future and their world (which is known as Beck's Negative Cognitive Triad). These distortions are thought to arise from early traumatic experiences, and CBT seeks to change the negative thoughts. CBT may be useful if the perceptions of the youngster with TS are very negative and persist in the face of other evidence to the contrary. Again, this would have to involve a skilled therapist who understood TS as well as the specific therapeutic techniques.

Behavioural therapies

Behaviour therapy is based upon learning theory and essentially concentrates on changing behaviour, and is thus directive in nature. Specific techniques include exposure, response prevention, habituation and thought stopping. Behaviour therapy may be particularly useful in treating the OCB/OCD aspects of a child with TS.

Pharmacological management

The biology of TS has been thoroughly reviewed, and many areas of the brain, such as frontal areas (the areas of planning and inhibiting behaviours), the basal ganglia (the seat of movements in the brain) and the limbic system (the seat of emotion in the brain) have been implicated in the cause of TS. Many neurotransmitters (chemicals in the brain which pass messages from nerve to nerve) have also been suggested as being important in TS. These include mainly dopamine, but also noradrenaline and serotonin. Medication is, at present, the mainstay of treatment of the actual motor and vocal tics of TS, as well as for some of the associated behaviours of TS, and the medications affect the chemicals most involved such as dopamine, noradrenaline and serotonin. Unless otherwise cited, much of this section has been obtained and modified for educationalists and allied professions from Robertson (2000).

The main medications used in TS include the typical neuroleptics (antipsychotics); atypical neuroleptics (antipsychotics); clonidine; antidepressants; and stimulants. These are described more fully below.

Neuroleptics (antipsychotics, major tranquillisers)

The most commonly prescribed medications for the motor and vocal tics have been the medications which block the biochemical **dopamine**, and the most successful agents in this group are called the typical neuroleptics, such as: haloperidol; pimozide; sulpiride, and tiapride.

It is important to understand that dopamine is the main biochemical also implicated in the illness called schizophrenia (a psychotic illness where patients may hear non-existent voices talking to them, or believe facts which are untrue, e.g. someone is conspiring against them), and that these medications are also used in the treatment of schizophrenia.

In this context, two things are important for the teacher to understand. Firstly, there is no connection whatsoever between TS and schizophrenia; and secondly, the doses of medications used for treating TS and schizophrenia differ widely (with the dose usually being very much smaller in TS). A dose of 20 milligrams (mg) of haloperidol a day would not be that uncommon in someone with a diagnosis of schizophrenia, but in TS the dose may be as low as 0.5 mg, and the daily dose is not recommended above 5–8 mgs (the doses of each medication are discussed overleaf).

The timing of taking the medications can also be important and can affect the functioning of pupils with TS. For example, with some of the neuroleptics, it may be possible to give only a single night time dose (so that the sedative side effects do not disturb the child during the day and may also assist with sleep).But for some children it may be necessary to give the tablets once, twice or even three times a day, and the mid-day dose may have to be taken at school.

Haloperidol

Haloperidol is one of the most widely used agents of treatment in TS. There have been many case reports of its successful use, as well as rigorous studies called double-blind trials (when neither the patient nor the doctor knows whether the patient is taking the active drug or the placebo [sugar pill]). In these trials haloperiodol has been shown to be superior to the placebo and/or its comparator agents. Unfortunately, haloperidol often produces unacceptable side effects in over three-quarters of patients taking the medication, and as a result there are many who discontinue its use. Thus if medications other than haloperidol are available they should probably be used as first line agents, not because they work better but because of haloperidol's excessive problematic side effects. The usual starting dose of haloperidol is 0.5 mg per day and it is increased by small amounts every week or so, depending on the response of the child's symptoms and the development of any side effects. A dose of 4 mg in children is probably the maximum with regards to efficacy and side effects.

Pimozide

Pimozide is another medication which blocks dopamine and which is also widely used in the treatment of TS. It has been shown to be effective in many double-blind trials and it is popular because of its relative lack of difficult side effects. Electrocardiogram (ECG) abnormalities (measurement of heart waves) have, however, been reported with pimozide and doctors therefore have to be cautious in prescribing it, and a baseline ECG is suggested before treatment, as is monitoring of the ECG during treatment. On the other hand, several studies have specifically reported no problems with cardiac side effects and pimozide.

As with haloperidol, the usual starting dose for pimozide is 0.5 mg per day and it is increased by small amounts every week or so, depending on the response of the symptoms and the development of any side effects. A dose of 4 mg in children is probably the optimal with regards to efficacy and side effects.

Sulpiride

The drug sulpiride is widely used in the UK for the treatment of motor and vocal tics, and is popular as it produces fewer extrapyramidal side effects (EPSEs) and less tardive dyskinesia (TD) (see p. 36). It is not made or licensed in the USA or Canada. It is probably one of the most popular medications in our clinic. In at least two studies we have published, sulpiride decreased motor and vocal tics, OCB, aggression and tension, and it also improved the patients' mood.

The average daily dose of sulpiride is between 400 and 800 mg. With children we often begin with a dose of 100 mg, i.e. half a tablet, and we increase the dose as necessary, depending on efficacy and side effects.

Tiapride

Tiapride is also useful in the treatment of the motor and vocal TS tics and it is widely used in Europe where it has been demonstrated to be better than comparator agents. It is not made nor licensed in the UK or USA.

Side effects

The side effects of the typical neuroleptics (antipsychotics) will be discussed in detail as they are not only important but may be subtle and unusual. In particular, the teacher in the classroom may well recognise some of them in pupils who are taking these medications. Twelve groups of the most common side effects of neuroleptics are described in the following section, and have been thoroughly reviewed in detail elsewhere. Unless otherwise indicated, the reference for the side effects is from Robertson (2000).

1. **Phobias and anxieties** such as school phobia and school avoidance have been brought on by neuroleptics (antipsychotics), especially haloperidol. In a well known paper on the subject, fifteen patients with TS (nine under the age of 16) developed school and work avoidance soon after commencement of treatment with low dose haloperidol (mean 2.5 mg per day) for a short period of time (mean 8 weeks). None of the children had experienced phobic symptoms before and were in fact relatively successful at school. The core symptoms were a persistent irrational fear of and compelling desire to avoid school. Children stayed at home or went to school very reluctantly. The symptoms disappeared with discontinuation or reduction of the drug (Mikkelsen *et al.* 1981).
2. **Cognitive effects**, which essentially means difficulties with concentration and attention, can also occur in children taking neuroleptics. This is serious as many children with TS, and particularly those who also have ADHD, already have inherent difficulties with concentration and attention.
3. **Drowsiness** is a particularly common side effect of neuroleptics and may be avoided by taking the medication at bedtime. We often tend to prescribe this type of medication at night, and when the child becomes used to it, it may be given in the daytime if necessary.

4. **Mood changes** can also be encountered in children taking neuroleptics. These include dysphoria (an internal feeling of discomfort and/or irritability), and depression. This may well be dose-related and thus the doctor can treat this symptom by reducing the dose, discontinuing the medication or, in some cases, by adding an appropriate antidepressant.

5. **Aggression** and hostility are reported side effects in a few children taking neuroleptics. With this symptom, there was a particular dose above which aggressive behaviour was encountered and below which the children were not aggressive (Bruun 1988).

6. **Akathisia** or restlessness (such as the feeling that the feet are shuffling and constantly on the go, or an internal restlessness) occurs in a substantial proportion of patients treated with neuroleptics, especially if the patient is neuroleptic naive, and it can also occur in individuals who have TS. It may be helped by neuroleptic dose reduction and withdrawal, or prescription of several of the 'antidote' medications.

7. **Increased appetite**, with a resultant weight increase, is common in patients treated with neuroleptics. The mechanism for this increase in weight is not fully understood. The doctor must, of course, rule out any other causes of weight gain. Strategies for overcoming the weight gain include dieting and taking regular healthy exercise.

8. **Dystonic** side effects are those resulting when a muscle or group of muscles become subjectively tight and the child may experience for example 'lock-jaw' or oculogyric crises (the subjectively very uncomfortable feeling of the eyes rolling upwards and backwards uncontrollably). There are medications such as procyclidine which act as 'antidotes' and counteract these side effects quickly and effectively. It is important to remember at this juncture that there are dystonic tics in TS, and that dystonia forms part of the differential diagnosis depending on the severity of the reaction.

9. **Extrapyramidal side effects** (EPSEs), named after the part of the nervous system they affect, are also known as Parkinsonian side effects, as they are similar to the symptoms seen in Parkinson's disease. These may include tremor, but are fairly rare at these low doses. They may be helped by decreasing the dose or by adding an 'antidote' medication.

10. **Tardive dyskinesia** (TD) is a side effect that consists of involuntary movements of the mouth and tongue (similar to those seen in old people who have removed their dentures). In general, it is not very common in TS patients treated with neuroleptics. Of importance, however, is that these tardive side effects have been reported in children exposed to even low doses of haloperidol. Unfortunately, treatment of this particular symptom is often quite difficult. Thankfully, this symptom is rarely of discomfort to the individual experiencing it, and it is more often distressing to the onlooker, be it a teacher or parent.

11. **ECG abnormalities** can occur with pimozide in particular, and this may deter some clinicians from prescribing it. If it is prescribed however, baseline ECG as well as regular ECG monitoring is recommended. In our clinic we do not use a lot of pimozide, but we always use regular and routine ECG monitoring.

12. **Endocrine** (gland) side effects can occur with neuroleptics. After puberty, sometimes young girls may lose their periods or have milk from their breasts, and young boys may have enlarged breasts with some neuroleptics.

Atypical neuroleptics

The relatively new or 'atypical' neuroleptics may be of potential use in children with TS, and the only one from this group which has been reported to do well in helping patients with TS in a large number of patients is risperidone. Risperidone affects **serotonin** and **dopamine** and it is thus an obvious choice for people with TS in which both these biochemicals have been implicated. Risperidone has been widely used and may be of theoretical benefit in TS especially if the patient has OCB, in which serotonin has been implicated. Risperidone has also been used in the treatment of individuals with ADHD. Reported results with this drug in people with TS have been more successful in the USA and Europe than in the UK.

Most reports use risperidone at a dose of 1.5 mg daily (range 0.5 to 4 mg); side effects may include drowsiness, dizziness, weight gain, anxiety and headaches.

Clonidine

Clonidine, which acts primarily on **noradrenalin**, has proved useful in treating TS, and it is of special use when the child with TS also has ADHD. Clonidine is conventionally taken as a tablet by mouth, but it can also be used as a patch on the skin. Many doctors worldwide now use clonidine. In our clinic it is the preferred drug for youngsters with both TS and ADHD. With clonidine not only the tics and ADHD respond but so do some of the other behaviours such as OCB, irritability, aggression, frustration and oppositional behaviours.

We start at a dose of 25 micrograms daily and build up the dose slowly to around 100-150 micrograms daily. It is usually given two to three times a day, depending on how it is tolerated by the child. There is also a clonidine patch which lasts for about a week. The drug takes about four weeks for its effects to be evident, but the maximal benefit may not be evident for about 4 to 6 months. A few patients do not respond, and a minority worsen on clonidine. Side effects of clonidine include drowsiness, dizziness, changes in mood (elated or depressed) and a slow pulse. It has been suggested that ECG, blood pressure and pulse monitoring should be carried out if clonidine is used.

Clonidine must not be discontinued fast, otherwise the child can experience a rebound increase in tics, or a dramatic rise in blood pressure.

Antidepressants

The antidepressants which have been used to treat various aspects of TS include the well established tricyclic antidepressants (TCAs) and the relatively new family of antidepressants called the selective serotonin reuptake inhibitors (SSRIs). Antidepressants have been used to treat the depression, the ADHD and the OCB aspects of TS. One of the main problems with the TCAs is the side effect profile which includes drowsiness, dry mouth, blurred vision, constipation, sweating and danger in overdose.

The SSRIs, on the other hand, are relatively free of adverse side effects. The SSRIs are also much safer in overdose (accidental or planned).

Stimulants

The use of stimulants in youngsters with TS has been controversial for some time, but they can be useful if used judiciously. The main stimulants used in children with TS include methylphenidate and dexamphetamine, which are the only ones licensed in the UK. Pemoline is licensed in the USA.

The use of methylphenidate (widely known as Ritalin) and dexamphetamine in children with TS and ADHD has long been controversial, as these stimulants may worsen the tics, while improving the hyperactivity and concentration. TS was once considered to represent a contra-indication, but now cautious use of these agents in TS has been advocated. Some studies have now been reported in which methylphenidate effectively decreased hyperactive and disruptive behaviours as well as physical aggression. Methylphenidate has inconsistent effects on tics. Methylphenidate only works for about four hours at a time. Thus, if the child takes the morning dose at 7 a.m., the effects will start wearing off at about 11 a.m. and the child will have to take the next dose then, so as to keep the medication working. The last dose should not be after 3 to 4 p.m., otherwise the child may have initial insomnia or disrupted sleep. It has been suggested that controlled release preparations may be helpful when treating ADHD with stimulants.

Less commonly used medications

Less commonly used medications which have been documented as useful in some patients with TS include tetrabenazine, the benzodiazepines, nicotine, calcium channel blockers, botulinum toxin injections, drugs which affect the opioid system, lithium, marijuana and melatonin (Robertson 2000), and these will be discussed briefly.

1. **Tetrabenazine** acts in two ways to alter dopamine, and it has been used succesfully in tic and hyperkinetic disorders especially in the USA and is used particularly by neurologists.

2. **The benzodiazepines** are a group of drugs of which diazepam (Valium) is probably the best known, was used in TS many years ago, but it may well only reduce the associated anxiety. We do not use this class of drugs in TS as there are problems with long term prescription, including addiction.

3. **Nicotine** may potentiate the effects of haloperidol in treating the effects of TS, but the only ways of using it successfully have included nicotine gum (nicorette) and nicotine patches. In our clinic we have not used any of these treatments as, apart from the questionable efficacy, we personally would not sanction the use of these products in children.

4. **Calcium channel blockers** have also been used with some success in treating TS patients. These include nifedipine, verapimil and flunarizine. Treatment results in a reduction of motor and vocal tic severity and frequency, as well as reducing irritability, inner tension and compulsive symptoms.

5. **Botulinum toxin** administered in local injections has been used successfully in focal dystonia (muscle twisting such as wry neck) for some time, and more recently it has proved useful in TS, targeting the symptoms of blepharospasm (excessive eye blinking to such an extent that the eyes may appear shut), neck twisting and severe coprolalia (when the injection is into the area of the vocal cords). Although these may be useful, injections have only been given to a small number of TS patients.

6. **Drugs which affect the opioid system** include naltrexone and naloxone and a small number of these have been useful in reducing TS symptoms, especially tics. The addiction potential of these substances is one risk, another is the exacerbation of tics after sudden withdrawal or cessation of the drug.

7. **Lithium** is not commony used in TS but has been reported as being successful in a small number of patients. When a patient receives lithium the blood has to be checked regularly as the lithium level in the blood has to be kept within a narrow range. Also, thyroid and kidneys functions have to be monitored, as they can be adversely affected by lithium.

8. **Marijuana** has been useful in reducing motor and vocal tics of some people with TS. Its effect may be to reduce the stress and anxiety that occurs secondary to TS, but also there have been suggestions that cannabinoids (drugs/chemicals which belong chemically to the marijuana family) may increase the effectiveness of neuroleptics in TS.

9. **Melatonin** may be useful for children with TS and ADHD who have problems with sleep, especially in getting off to sleep. In these children, and in the few cases documented to date there seem to be no significant serious side effects (Freeman 1997).

Administration of medication in school hours

It is often difficult to decide who should administer the medication to children during school hours. Parents are responsible for their children's treatment until they reach the age of 16 years. There is no legal age limit below which a child cannot look after his or her prescribed medication. In the majority of instances it would be unsafe for the child to take care of the tablets. Thus it is wisdom rather than law that dictates who should look after the child's medication. It is best for the doctor who prescribes the medication to discuss in detail with the parents the logistics of the child taking the medication (i.e. frequency, actual times) and for the parents, in turn, to share this information with the person at school who will look after the medication. Many youngsters with TS are very well informed about their medication and when it has to be taken, and in these cases it may be appropriate for the tablets to be looked after by someone in authority, but for the child to have the empowerment of sharing with the adult caretaker the responsibility of remembering the medication timetable.

There is no official guidance about who is the most appropriate person to look after or administer the medication of the young pupil with TS. Such individuals may include:

- the head teacher
- the class teacher or form teacher
- the school nurse
- the school matron
- the school bursar
- the school secretary
- the parents/carers.

In many instances the doctors will prescribe medications which can be given as a once night-time dose, thus not having to involve the school at all. This may involve a neuroleptic and the side effect may be sedation, but this may well be useful in children who have initial insomnia. Other medications such as methylphenidate (Ritalin) will have to be taken during school hours.

Psychosurgery

In a very few cases of individuals with TS who have severe motor and vocal tics and who, usually, have severe OCS/OCB and SIB as well, psychosurgery has been used successfully. However, as there have been fewer than 40 such operations ever performed on TS patients, a very formalised approach has been suggested (Rauch *et al.* 1995).

Chapter 6

Developing and Valuing the Individual

What is critical to later adaptation is the child's sense of himself or herself as competent and loved. (Cohen *et al*. 1988)

Teachers are central in helping pupils with TS to experience schooling positively and enabling them to acquire those competencies that will allow them to cope successfully, not only at school but throughout adult life, despite their puzzling and unpredictable disorder. The associated behavioural symptoms such as obsessions, compulsions, irritability, low threshold of frustration, impulsive behaviour and hyperactivity which can contribute to learning difficulties present particular challenges for teachers, and the way they react has a critical impact both on pupils' opinions of themselves and of others. Shimberg (1995) has described it fittingly: 'Confidence and positive self-image require careful and constant nurturing. In the beginning, it means more effort for an already busy teacher, but in the long run, it creates a more disciplined and pleasing environment – for all children.'

Often the biggest hurdles for teachers are determining where the boundaries lie between the TS and a pupil's voluntary disruptive or defiant behaviour, what is reasonable to accommodate and where to set the limits. Concerns shared with colleagues and contacts made with other professionals let teachers feel more supported and skilled.

Teachers are sometimes the first to recognise a pupil's symptoms of TS and can make a major impact on persuading pupils to unlock their own strengths and abilities by giving them the tools and opportunities. The school day is often pressurised and although demands on pupils and staff are numerous, teachers make huge efforts to boost pupils' self-esteem and communication skills. School personnel are diligent and are constantly trying to do more for their pupils. However, alone, few can meet pupils' diverse SEN and they need understanding and encouragement so that they do not inadvertently convey their frustrations to the pupil.

Raising pupils' self-esteem and self-confidence

All pupils achieve more when they are motivated, understand what is expected of them, feel secure enough to concentrate on their work and let go of extraneous anxieties. This includes pupils with TS, many of whom function satisfactorily in school without extra assistance. For those who have more extreme disorders, extra educational interventions are essential to build up their personal and practical skills. Such imputs are necessary to enable them to enhance these vital academic and interpersonal skills by:

- managing anxiety
- strengthening self-confidence
- augmenting socialisation skills
- developing abilities to focus and concentrate
- reducing impulsive responses
- improving organisational skills
- acquiring compensatory techniques to help them achieve more, particularly in areas such as handwriting, reading and maths.

Alongside others in the fields of medicine and education, we who work regularly with youngsters with TS have found that it is not necessarily the tics that cause them the most distress at school. It is often the ostracism and rejection by others, who do not comprehend that it is the involuntary nature of TS and associated behaviour such as ADHD, that can erode their self-esteem (Packer 1997, Wolff 1988, Hagin *et al.* 1982).

In a study of individuals with TS at the severe end of the spectrum research has shown that a number of them went on to have difficulties in social adaptation in later life (Robertson *et al.* 1997). Pupils who feel secure, valued and confident at school will find themselves much more favourably positioned to participate actively in school life and later in the wider community.

Key areas for skill building

Some key areas where teachers can work with pupils to help them build up their personal and practical skills are:

- developing pupils' communication and relationship skills
- finding ways to boost their self-esteem
- harnessing developments in Information and Communication Technology (ICT) to help pupils with poor writing skills
- simplifying complex instructions and reinforcing the information
- arranging a safe time-out space – a refuge – when a pupil may need to withdraw without seeking specific permission
- modifying arrangements for timed tests and exams which provoke anxiety
- dividing work into smaller steps to suit pupils' slower pace.

Some pupils with TS will need a focused approach such as an Individual Education Plan (IEP) to gain the most from these opportunities (DFE 1994).

Schools that provide pupils with such openings are meeting the fundamental aims of the National Curriculum (DfEE 1999): to provide opportunities for all pupils to learn and achieve, to promote their spiritual, moral, social and cultural development and prepare them for the opportunities, responsibilities and experiences of life.

Pain caused by peer rejection

Healthy self-esteem gives an individual a secure sense of identity and the ability to acknowledge and value his own efforts and achievements. Feeling good about oneself enhances self-confidence, optimism and willingness to interact with others, without losing sight of the importance of enjoying one's own company. Positive experiences promote positive self-esteem, and the disruptive behaviour some pupils with TS display in school may be symptomatic of the damage they have already suffered to their self-esteem. Children who have TS are usually quite aware of their tics and noises and sufficiently sensitive enough to be aware of the reactions of others to them. This leaves them feeling 'different, unaccepted, and left out and their self-esteem may suffer' as Kaplan (1992) has described.

Links between poor self-image and low attainment are increasingly being recognised officially in government documents. 'Improvements in behaviour are more likely to follow if the child's self-esteem can be enhanced, and if the pupil can be brought to recognise the effects of his or her behaviour' (DFE 1994a). Similarly, adults need positive self-esteem to be successful. Those schools where personnel feel valued and appreciated are often the more welcoming and affirming of all pupils.

Pupils with TS are no different. Most of them can operate in school satisfactorily, but those who have experienced discrimination because of personal characteristics over which they have no control, like their involuntary noises or tics, may often be reluctant to expose themselves to further risk, or to new circumstances. The fact that symptoms can be suppressed for short spells may exacerbate the confusion about the precise nature of the disorder and may reduce adults' and peers' sympathy. When pupils have come to regard themselves as stupid or worthless, they are less likely to keep on trying in case they fail and experience yet again all those dismal feelings associated with failure. They may then become defiant: refusing to start a task or feeling too shy to try, rushing the task to get it over with or neglecting to pay attention, believing that they cannot succeed.

The pain caused by such rejection is explicit in a poem written by 17-year-old Jason Valencia, who has TS (Shimberg 1995):

Maybe I spit, maybe I swear,
or constantly tap my hand.
How do I explain these things to you,
when I, myself, don't understand.

Yes, it hurts me deep inside
When I hear the taunting words you say.

In more extreme, but certainly not unusual cases, pupils with TS will act the fool or become verbally or physically aggressive. This allows them to avoid being shown up yet again as either being unable to do a task at all – for example, replying in French, or not doing it as well as their ideal self desires, e.g. drawing a neat diagram in science. These pupils who may have phonic tics or poor fine motor skills would rather deliberately refuse to do work or to be seen to behave very badly, than show they cannot do the work adequately.

A child's phonic tics when they are first vocalised may disrupt the classroom resulting in teasing and social rejection by peers, leaving the child isolated and withdrawn. Such feelings are often hard to acknowledge and to express appropriately unless the pupil feels accepted by others and can trust them. Empathetic and sensitive responses by school personnel working in partnership with parents will help the child dismantle his defences. The more affirmative the statements pupils with TS can hear about themselves from as many different sources, the greater their chances will be of recovering from damaged self-esteem. Pupils with more severe forms of TS may feel intense frustration, anger and pain about their impairment.

Case Study: Jake

JAKE in Year Six interrupted literacy lessons when he constantly made loud throat clearing noises while his teacher was reading aloud. He would then often tap his pencil on the table during the follow-up group working sessions. His classmates tried to ignore him until one day he started shaking the table as well. Jason sitting next to him jumped up, yelled and grabbed his shoulder. The learning support assistant (LSA) intervened swiftly. She suggested quietly that Jason should go and have a drink of water and then talk to the class teacher. She took Jake outside. He sobbed despairingly about his embarrassment and fears. She comforted him and they agreed to discuss his concerns with his group. They came up with these solutions:

Jake would ask his teacher if he could take home a text she was going to read with the whole class, so that he could read it in advance because when he had to concentrate hard on new material and read aloud his tics frequently got worse. He would not be expected to read aloud, but could stand and use the pointer for the class to follow the words. Several times a week instead of handwriting the follow-up tasks, he would write on the word processor with a different classmate.

Classroom activity: Putting-ups instead of putting-downs.
Swapping put-ups encourages pupils to substitute put-downs they might make about one another with complimentary put-ups. They could do this verbally in Circle Time or in Personal, Social, Health Education (PSHE) sessions or could write them in a language lesson. Each child thinks of three put-ups to say or write about a pupil (for example) sitting on their left. There needs to be some order so that each pupil receives a few put-ups and no-one is left out. They write these down and then exchange them or tell them to their neighbours. If children can't yet write or don't wish to, they could draw three put-ups. There can also be displays of put-ups boards in the classroom for pupils to pin up a put-up about someone else, or, of course, about themselves.

As the work of Mosley and Tew (1999) has shown the circle process successfully promotes dialogue between the subgroups that form within a class. When there are no put-downs youngsters can relax and become more willing to tolerate others' individuality and empathise. Twenty minutes or so weekly or fortnightly of Circle Time to let pupils voice their ideas about school issues that have arisen or will arise can provide welcome safety valves for pupils with TS, who despite teachers' or tutors' best efforts frequently come up against obstacles to their inclusion and learning.

Extra access to ICT for pupils who have difficulties with handwriting and fine motor skills can help them greatly to function independently and produce work that is commensurate with their abilities.

For those considerable numbers of pupils with TS/OCB/OCD, who may also have learning difficulties, the pressure to produce work which they themselves feel is inferior, and within a specific time scale, can fuel their desire to respond inappropriately in order to guard their own feelings of self-worth. Allowing pupils with TS extra time to finish tasks or tests helps them compensate for the time lost to tics, obsessional thoughts or compulsive behaviour. If others complain about unfair advantages, this could be a cue for some PSHE and Citizenship lessons on understanding that individuals have different needs, cultures and beliefs that deserve to be treated with respect.

Pre-arranging breaks from the class is essential. Warning cues such as increased sniffing or throat clearing may signal that a pupil needs to withdraw to regain a sense of control. By unambiguously showing understanding, adults reinforce in the pupil the feeling that he is accepted and has his behaviour under control. This in turn reduces his inner pain at his involuntary behaviour, over which he has so little control. Over time this can reduce pent-up feelings of despair or anger, especially against his own body. Putting any pressure on children to repress their tics is counter-productive, as the stress involved will diminish the energy they have for learning and their emotions can then erupt in subsequent frustration.

Classroom activity: Recognising and naming emotions.
We know that many children lack the adequate vocabulary to explain their feelings. One quick way to extend this knowledge can take place at the end of a language lesson. Provide a pile of cards with one emotion written or illustrated on each. Working in their groups each pupil picks one that best describes how he or she is feeling and has a turn to mime the emotion to the others, who then guess what the emotion is. In another ten-minute slot at another time the pupils share feedback on which emotions are harder to portray and why, and provide suggestions on how this could be made easier. Ideas for words on cards for older pupils: carefree, relaxed, furious, miserable, downcast. For non-readers drawings or photos could be substituted.

The tendency amongst a number of pupils with TS to self-injure, as mentioned earlier, can threaten their health and even their lives and may compound peer rejection or ostracism. This in turn can incite them to further outbursts of aggressive behaviour and they can end up refusing to go to school, or being excluded.

Providing support during transition

Change is a challenging time for all. For pupils who have TS/ADHD/OCD and low self-confidence, transfers to different schools can very unsettling, and close cooperation between school and homes will ease such change. Early contact with parents is critical for a school to start planning and be ready to provide early intervention if necessary. Pupils who come into a school mid-year or outside the main intake period may also find settling in very troublesome and struggle to make friends.

Children who are likely to be most upset and 'at risk' at transition times have or have experienced:

- irregular attendance patterns
- poor social skills and peer relationships
- withdrawn behaviour
- low self-esteem
- difficulties with the curriculum and behavioural problems
- emotional instability. (DfEE 1999)

Children with TS integrating or re-integrating from specialist provision or home tuition often need additional learning and pastoral support to boost their basic skills before transition. Preliminary visits to their intended schools will help children prepare emotionally and mentally.

Understanding and taming anger

A quick temper and angry outbursts can undermine the most determined effort to help youngsters nurture their self-image and self-esteem. For pupils with TS anger is inevitably a secondary emotion arising from primary emotions such as fear, embarrassment, frustration, jealousy, and even grief that are linked to their disorder.

Hansen (1992) has indicated that for about 25 to 35 per cent of children with TS controlling aggression or temper tantrums is a problem and leads them into fights for little or no reason, yet leaves them feeling remorseful between outbursts. Although such eruptions may appear to have no cause, anger is always a reaction to something. Such outbursts in the classroom may not even be in response to an actual event, but may be a pupil's reaction to her perception about what has occurred.

Case Study: Sarah

SARAH saw her best friend Kelly handing out pink envelopes to three girls one morning. She recalled painful occasions in her previous school in another part of the country where she had been excluded from classmates' parties and discos because of her coprolalia. Although in her new school she felt accepted the pretty envelopes triggered harsh memories. Sarah perceived that Kelly had arranged a party and was not going to invite her. She had to try hard to muffle the swear words that repeatedly tormented her that day. She refused to have lunch with Kelly, who was hurt but persisted in talking to her. Later on as they were leaving school, Kelly asked Sarah if she could borrow her Bart Simpson outfit as she, Grace, Pasha and Esther had been invited by their former head teacher to put on an act at their old local primary school to help raise funds for a new hall. 'Is that what was in the fake – fake – fake pink envelopes?' Sarah blurted out before she could even try to stop herself. She turned red in embarrassment. Kelly gazed at her friend for a few moments. Then a cloud lifted and she realised what had been troubling Sarah all day.

The challenge for adults is to teach the pupil how to intervene more successfully at the trigger stage when they sense sudden mental or physiological changes, which they recognise, can lead to aggressive outbursts. Timing matters: the earlier the intervention, the more effective. Children with TS often need assistance from professional agencies such as the educational psychology service to help them pinpoint what arouses these powerful emotions and how to cope with them.

Anger can arise from bewilderment about situations that are unfair, stressful or unjust and when expressed it can effectively provide opportunities for learning, change and regaining self-control. Educational psychologists Faupel *et al.* (1998) have shown how expressions of anger in school if responded to constructively can improve insights and relationships and situations that would otherwise remain troubling.

Long-term planning and implementation of anger management programmes are essential, and whole-school policies for reactions to crises and aggressive outbursts that are consistently followed by all school personnel are the most effectual. Once initiatives have been explained to pupils, they need to be absolutely familiar with their options.

Acquiring skills to handle anger

Preventative measures that can be learned by pupils with TS are:

- to identify triggers for their anger, i.e. when they see something happening or remember something that has made them angry in the past
- to recognise the subsequent feelings as cues to avoid responding aggressively
- to cope with the explosive feelings
- to take steps that will prevent them reacting in damaging ways.

Small steps that may assist a child with TS to keep anger under control are:

- walking away
- distracting oneself with another task or going to play somewhere else
- talking to someone trustworthy about the angry feelings

- thinking of something enjoyable that has happened or will soon happen
- drinking water
- seeking support
- taking pre-arranged time out in a safe place
- breathing deeply and slowly to help reduce the physiological arousal that accompanies the build of anger
- writing about one's feelings or drawing in an 'Anger Diary'.

Pupils can be encouraged to acquire habits that will help them contain their angry feelings when they feel them mounting in the classroom. During whole-class sessions let them have an object to help dissipate these emotions – for example, a soft toy or string of worry beads to fiddle with, or a piece of plasticene to mould. When they feel their tics might become disruptive to others, they know they can move to somewhere neutral: to sit on a cushion, to go to the toilet.

When a pupil is genuinely stuck and will only become increasingly frustrated if expected to do an assignment he cannot do unaided, the following steps could be tried when an adult is not immediately available to give extra help: Ask a peer for help. Then spend five to ten minutes trying again. Put a mark on the board signalling to adults or peers that you have tried these steps and remain stuck. A peer can then come over and give assistance, or an adult will come as soon as possible. In infant classes you can use a short clothesline on which the child pegs up his name. This is removed when he gets help. While pupils wait, alternative worksheets can be attempted or non-readers can look at books.

If you have to move any pupil away from his peers in the classroom as a last resort tactic to signify that his behaviour is not acceptable, or to provide some quiet time for those around him, ask another pupil to go and sit next to him. Often the pupil who has been disruptive will disrupt more if he has to sit alone, but if he sits apart with someone else, he may well conform again. This is not unfair to peers as long as different peers are asked to move with him and it only happens occasionally. It does, however, sometimes suit some pupils to go and sit alone for a while. When the pupil returns to the group, try to give some silent affirmatory signal. A smile gives the pupil that essential message that he is liked and welcome alongside his peers. It only takes 14 muscles to smile at him, and 72 to frown (Loomans 1996). It may be unwise to try to resort to humouring a pupil with TS who is on the point of losing her temper, though it can be done successfully. Pupils who frequently experience angry feelings badly desire adult support in removing the causes of their anger.

Dealing with pupils who have short fuses can be very stressful. Staff and parents/carers need to take steps to receive support for their own emotional wellbeing, so that they do not become drained but can keep their roles in perspective.

Chapter 7

Forming Good Relationships

If you're thinking you're acting happy but actually seem too hyper or angry, you find other kids getting angry at you in turn, and you don't realize why. Such kids end up feeling no sense of control over how other people treat them, that their actions have no impact on what happens to them. It leaves them feeling powerless, depressed, and apathetic.

(Stephen Nowicki in Goleman 1996)

Relationships with others decisively influence a pupil's self-esteem and pupils who have TS may repeatedly have suffered failures in social interactions which have dramatically lowered their self-confidence. The extreme symptoms of TS, such as loud vocal tics or unusual motor tics such as licking, can cause classmates of these pupils to avoid or tease them so retarding the advance of their social skills. This can lead in extreme cases to psychological problems such as deep-seated anxieties, depression and increased tendencies to withdraw, suggesting that TS is not only a disorder of tics but is a complex disorder affecting many areas of psychological and interpersonal function, which together have a major influence on peer relationships (Stokes *et al*, 1991). Often this results in social isolation for many individuals who have TS, as Riddle *et al*. have documented (1988).

Wolff (1988) has found that the suffering that individuals with TS undergo is mainly experienced – with the exception of rare instances of physically hurtful tics – in the interpersonal field and that some youngsters with TS may suffer from all or any of the usual neurotic complaints of life but because of their disorder many have 'less ego strength to deal with the neuroses of everyday life'.

Pupils with TS at risk of becoming seriously disaffected and spiralling down into refusing to attend or being excluded from school may have had:

- low self-esteem and poor relationships with peers
- unauthorised attendance and extended truancy problems
- a history of behavioural difficulties at school
- emotional instability
- difficulty with the curriculum.

Links between low self-esteem, poor communication abilities and disaffection

49

Multi-agency approaches can support schools to help those pupils with these issues. The Education Welfare Service (EWS), educational psychologists, health workers, social services departments, youth service and child and adolescent mental health services all make distinct contributions. The work of multi-disciplinary groupings such as Youth Offending Teams (YOTs) covering pupil absenteeism, exclusion and provision for pupils out of school is explained in the DfEE Circular 10/99 entitled *Social Inclusion: Pupil Support*.

Pupils who do not respond to efforts by their school to overcome disaffection are at serious risk of being permanently excluded. Recognising that such vulnerable pupils may require a programme of more detailed support to modify their behaviour, the UK Government reacted recently by introducing school-based Pastoral Support Programmes (PSPs) that involve multi-agency intervention (DfEE 10/99). A PSP will be automatically set up for a pupil who has had several fixed period exclusions that may lead to a permanent exclusion, or who has been otherwise identified as being at risk of failure at school through disaffection.

A *whole-school approach to bullying*

Peer behaviour such as belittling or singling out a pupil with a disability, name calling and bullying or, alternatively, deliberate ignoring inevitably inflicts much suffering. Frequently underlying these attitudes are prejudices and assumptions that inflict more damage on pupils' self-esteem than TS itself and can interfere with the development of age-appropriate interpersonal and academic proficiencies. Packer (1997) has recorded that rejection by peers and those who do not understand the involuntary nature of TS was cited by children and adolescents in their conversations with her as the greatest impact felt. Burd and Kerbeshian (1992) have suggested that 'social skill deficiencies are common in children with TS and are often overlooked' and therefore compensatory programmes should be the focus of intervention programmes for children with TS, who may also have learning and behavioural difficulties. They have found that many of the negative behaviours seen in pupils with TS result from pupils' lack of an alternative positive social repertoire.

All bullying is unacceptable. Children with TS whose symptoms such as motor and vocal tics are obvious can be particularly victimised by bullies. We know of children who have been nicknamed 'Noddy' or 'Nudge Nudge Wink Wink'. Children who are so teased require a substantial amount of encouragement to re-build their self-confidence with their peers, especially if it has led to their reluctance or refusal to attend school. Bullying is often difficult to spot as most bullying tends to take place outside the classroom, and all adults in schools should remain vigilant to watch out for signs, to act promptly and firmly in order to help safeguard victims *and* bullies. Pupils with TS learn to view failure by adults to respond as tacit toleration.

There has been much coverage in the medical literature recently about bullying, suggesting that there may be physical characteristics of victims that allow them to become particularly prone to being bullied (Voss and Mulligan 2000). Bullying may result in depression and anxiety (Salmon 1998). Children with moderate to severe TS with obvious tics may therefore be especially vulnerable to being bullied and may then become depressed and anxious.

Many pupils who repeatedly experience difficulties in their relationships lack the vocabulary and language skills to express themselves in ways commonly acceptable to others. Research has consistently pointed to the importance of talk in children's learning, both at home and at school; yet the evidence indicates that the quantity and the quality of such interaction between adults and children in many settings tend to be poor (DfEE 1997). There are some language problems fairly common to pupils with TS, such as the repetition of words and sounds, and this might sound like stuttering. Their classmates may whisper or say inappropriate or swear words that the pupils with TS may involuntarily mimic and it is necessary for adults to be aware of the possibility of this kind of subtle provocation. Schools should view it as a priority to address issues related to language difficulties by collaborating with other professionals who can provide specialist advice and support.

Promoting language and socialisation skills

> *Classroom activity: A three-step approach can be taught to children from a very early age to start empowering them to look after themselves.*
> A child who has coprolalia is often teased and bullied. The child could be supported to say: 'I do not like it when you copy my words, as I can't help it when I say them. You make me feel very miserable/unhappy when you say that. I want you to stop'. This is undoubtedly a very tall order for a child and it would certainly not be appropriate for all children in all circumstances, but for those with a certain level of maturity it is worth trying.
> This kind of activity can easily be fitted into a PSHE scheme of work.

All schools have a statutory responsibility to provide their pupils with a curriculum for personal, social and health education. There is already much in the new Department for Education and Employment (DfEE) frameworks for PSHE and Citizenship to give schools a basis for developing their existing approaches flexibly. Schools are encouraged to ensure the entitlement to PSHE of all pupils with SEN and to give all pupils chances to reflect on their own strengths and weaknesses, share and discuss ideas, negotiate targets and communicate effectively with others. The National Healthy School Standard (NHSS) launched in 1999 supports the effective implementation of these frameworks. These new initiatives provide ideas for teachers to make the most of all kinds of cross-curricular activities to focus on the 'emotional fabric of a child's life', as Goleman (1996) has called it, and so raise the level of social and emotional competence in all children as an integral part of their every day education and not just as an extra curriculum for children with SEN.

Opportunities for showing and dealing with emotions

Classroom activity: Reflective exercises for developing ways to sustain a new friendship.
1. Brainstorm different types of friendly relationships.
2. Count the numbers of times different kinds of acquaintances and friends met during the week or over a month.
3. Analyse whether the number and quality of friendships they have made with a new friend have been reciprocated.
4. Reflect on any mismatches and how these could be balanced.
5. Role-play ways of asking about another's feelings.
6. Encourage observations of body language and cues.
7. Play listening games to strengthen ways of really listening to a friend without discounting what he might say.

Pupils with low self-esteem who have difficulties relating to peers and adults in school benefit from all opportunities to discuss and role play in particular where these involve:

- identifying and naming their own feelings
- evaluating beforehand the likely consequences of their behaviour on others
- adapting to unfamiliar and unexpected situations
- recognising and responding to body language and cues
- changing their behaviour to remain safe and successful in new situations
- generating alternative solutions to difficulties.

Classroom activity: Opportunities to respond to non-verbal cues.
- Arrange pupils into small groups according to their favourite TV series. Ask them to choose some recent incidents and discuss scenes from it, focusing on the characters' emotions, cues and responses. Some clothes or props can help them overcome any shyness and can improve the quality of interpretation.
- Let them predict how they would feel if they were part of the scene and then discuss similarities with recent real events in their lives.
- Ask them to explore how their own feelings can provide clues to how others might be feeling.
- Suggest they each write down one insight they have gained and how it might benefit them.
- Give them an opportunity in a week's time to recount anything they might have tried as an outcome of this exercise.

To succeed and to feel relaxed in social settings, pupils with TS/ADHD often need a lot of help to learn to comprehend and interpret a number of social cues simultaneously and accurately.

Promoting social skills in lessons

Teachers need to use every opportunity provided by lesson time to promote the social skills of pupils with TS/ADHD.

- Show pupils with TS/ADHD who are naturally impulsive how to acquire habits such as becoming a bit more patient, sharing properly and letting others speak first. This is fundamental in demonstrating the relationship between their choices of behaviour and how others treat them.
- Encourage them to concentrate on what they are hearing and not just on waiting to chip in with their own ideas, points of view or demands. Youngsters with TS often could do with more prompting to remember cause and effect and the benefits of really listening to others.
- Issue frequent reminders to use quieter voice levels in the classroom – children with TS/ADHD tend to speak loudly.
- Encourage them to invent their own affirmatory symbols or complimentary slips to give to their peers and let them also practise confirming their own efforts.
- Give instructions one or two steps at a time and when possible go to the pupil with TS and quietly check that he has understood the instruction.
- Try suggesting to a pupil who mutters to himself while working that he move to a desk where others cannot hear him, but arrange this beforehand privately with him.
- Be sensitive to pupils' favoured learning styles, maybe working with a partner rather than with a group. Collaboration with others can stimulate them to take risks with their learning, which they might not do on their own.
- Say 'yes' as often as possible to pupils' requests. Children with TS often view school more negatively than their peers who don't have any physically limiting disorders. Stay flexible: responding positively to their reasonable – if unplanned for – requests can help redress this balance.
- Say 'no' calmly and consistently and, when necessary, briefly explain why. This will allow children to understand the reasons, so enhancing their feelings of security, and build up recognition of boundaries.
- Avoid providing Hobson's choices which can lead to mistrust of adult intentions, such as 'If you choose to go on disturbing Peter, you will have to stay in at break to finish your maths'. Instead try 'Now it's time, Wesley to get on with your maths, so that you will be able to go out to break with Peter'. In other words, do not let him think that choosing to continue disturbing Peter is a viable choice.
- Give unambiguous directions to help pupils with TS/ADHD: 'Now it's time to. . .' rather than 'If you choose to go on . . . then you will. . .'.

Working in groups and staying friends

Many of the National Curriculum activities require pupils to work collaboratively with others. Pupils with TS often experience difficulties here (Stokes 1991) and because of the nature of their disorder, can be ostracised by others when groups are chosen.

It is helpful to involve pupils in drawing up some rules for working collaboratively with others such as these guidelines for effective group working in secondary schools.

- Try and make eye contact, be sensitive to body cues and address others by name.
- Be sensitive to those who feel shy in a group and encourage those who might want to dominate to listen more.
- Avoid mimicking, mocking, judging and talking too much.
- Focus on the topic under discussion.
- Address questions to the whole group, not only to your friends.
- Express your own feelings and ask for clarification if you don't understand.
- Challenge others' views in friendly ways but do respect confidentiality.
- Apologise if you cause offence, hurt or upset someone.

Promoting social skills during lunch breaks

Although most youngsters prefer to work or play with others, children who have vocal or motor tics are frequently embarrassed and isolated when spending time with others. When they do become emotional or tearful or angry after a group session, an adult or a reliable peer needs to offer support. LSAs and Midday Supervisory Assistants (MSAs) are often well positioned to help children develop communication skills. They can create situations and initiate conversations informally giving pupils opportunities to see that others can also feel vulnerable.

The following steps can help:

- Stay calm. Tears or anger can bring relief and the pupil may feel more in control of himself for having been able to cry or having an angry verbal outburst.
- Move to a quieter place and offer reassurance.
- Encourage the pupil to talk about what is upsetting him. If he finds this difficult, ask him if you can arrange for him to talk to another adult.
- Don't ignore his tears. It is always reassuring to others to recognise that someone is willing to intervene when a pupil is clearly distressed.
- Be sympathetic to your own body language and avoid adopting a stiff posture.
- On a subsequent occasion if another pupil becomes emotional, try involving the pupil with TS in offering support. This allows him to empathise with others and share the skills he has been acquiring in receiving and giving support.

Play and break times may be made easier and more enjoyable if some advance planning is done. In particular, have plans for those pupils with TS who may need extra support during breaks, as these can be critical times of stress for many youngsters. Explore the flexibility of allowing vulnerable children to spend some time indoors at break with one or several friends, playing games that involve social skills such as turn taking, playing fairly, losing decently. Take the opportunity of teaching them playground games, play with them and invite others to join.

Don't make threats that won't then be carried out, try not to respond differently at different times to the same behaviour and check that requests are obeyed.

It can be useful to keep a dressing up box and a box of puppets for dramatisation. Often pupils with tics or obsessions, that can exaggerate feelings of self-consciousness, can lose themselves wearing a hat or feather boa pretending to be someone else. Playing disco music outdoors once a week for 15 minutes can work wonders. Children with motor or phonic tics that interrupt their classroom learning frequently find them no barrier to dancing, playing a musical instrument or participating in sport. It is well known that tics frequently reduce or disappear when children are involved in one of these activities.

Chapter 8

Focusing on Positive Behaviour

What a difference real understanding can make! All the well-meaning advice in the world won't amount to a hill of beans if we're not even addressing the real problem. And we'll never get to the problem if we're so caught up in our own autobiography, our own paradigms, that we don't take off our glasses long enough to see the world from another point of view.
(Covey 1990)

When teaching or supporting pupils who have TS it is important to resist noticing the tics and the sniffs or the distracted behaviour and instead concentrate on the whole child. Intermittent, impulsive strange sounds often disturb a lesson. The more they can be ignored, the more the whole class will benefit and gradually may over time not even notice them. This will greatly advantage the child who has TS, as studies have shown repeatedly that lack of stress frequently leads to reduced tics or other outbursts. Pupils who have TS and an identified specific learning or behavioural difficulty progress best when there are specific programmes in place to help them overcome these.

Aggressive behaviour in the classroom

Aggression towards others is a major behavioural symptom linked with TS and its associated behaviours and might in more extreme cases be expressed in distressing ways such as yelling, biting, scratching and destroying work. Such conduct can be socially disabling for the individuals as it is extremely disturbing for others present, even though it is usually more threatening than actually harmful to them. School friends begin to ostracise such a pupil fearing what might happen to them. Such outbursts might also provoke bullying, as pupils taunt to evoke an aggressive outburst knowing that their peer with TS might get irritable easily and lash out voluntarily or involuntarily.

Case Study: Katie

KATIE aged eight was listening with three classmates to an audio cassette and following instructions to draw a rain forest. They were told to find a red pencil. Unfortunately there were only three on the table. Before Katie could pick one, the others had taken the pencils. 'I just became so angry, so quickly because I wanted a red pencil. They took them and I had to wait. So I scribbled black all over my drawing, ran into the cloakroom and threw their coats onto the floor. When Miss came, I started to cry because I was really sorry but I don't know why I did it. Something just goes flash in my head and I can't stop myself'.

Feeling out of control like this creates great anxiety, as a pupil knowing she has behavioural difficulties, fears she cannot control her frightening behaviour. Riddle *et al.* (1988) have found that for some the feeling of being out of control can even exceed the expression of the behavioural symptoms and the tics. A negative school and classroom environment significantly affects the performance and behaviour of the student with TS/ADHD and/or OCB/OCD. If the pupil does not feel emotionally safe to make mistakes and express involuntary symptoms, he inevitably experiences anxiety, frustration, anger and stress (Dornbush and Pruitt 1993).

Focusing on the essentials

After a pupil with TS has been implicated in a distressing incident, have a private brief meeting with the pupil. Do this when he is feeling cooperative, not when he is feeling threatened, has lowered self-esteem or would rather be on the playground. Discuss his insights into the incidents and the effects of his behaviour on others. Ask him *what* happened, not *why* he behaved inappropriately. The 'why?' questions may not elicit a response from children, who often find themselves in trouble for a variety of confusing reasons.

Strategies for repairing emotional hurt will need to be worked out with the pupil. Empower the pupil to offer solutions for repairing the situation. Take seriously what he suggests, incorporate his suggestions and encourage him to take ownership of joint responsibility with the teacher for modifying his behaviour.

- If appropriate introduce — or review – a behavioural modification plan or an Individual Education Plan and agree new or continuing targets linked to his age and maturity. Confirm any rewards or consequence systems.
- Provide a structured routine for him to follow as far as possible and try to give him some advance notice when there are going to be major disruptions to class schedules.
- Clarify arrangements for time-out or for seeking help when he needs privacy to cope with his emotions or to express pent-up tics. The safe place could be the counsellor's office, the library, a resource room or a special chair in the classroom for young children. Privately pre-arrange with the pupil a hand signal that indicates the need to leave the classroom, or agree to allow the pupil to leave when necessary.
- Offer opportunities for counselling or emotional support.
- Explain to him ways of responding differently when provoked or feeling irritated. Let the pupil actually role-play some of this

so that he really feels confident about reacting differently. Do not underestimate the importance of this. Young pupils, especially, might not ever before have had one-to-one opportunities to rehearse such situations and try out different reactions when relating to others, e.g. turn taking, listening actively, and waiting patiently.

- Model respectful behaviour. If the adult displays empathy for a pupil, peers will manifest the same behaviour.
- Praise the pupils no matter how small the success.

All these steps will be much more successful if his parents back them and adversarial positions between school and home are avoided. Research from the US quoted in a leader article in the British Medical Journal identifies learning environments supported by positive parent–child relationships as one of the three key facets of effective child discipline. The other two are a strategy for systematically teaching and strengthening desired behaviours and a strategy of decreasing or eliminating undesired behaviours (Waterson 2000).

Pupils with TS who have poor interpersonal skills need to be taught how to turn confrontations into discussions or negotiation. If he says: 'I don't care', reply: 'Well, I do care. Now please listen to the instruction quietly'. Continue with the group and expect him to comply. If he says, 'You can't make me', agree. Then add calmly: 'but I can ask Mr James to escort you out of the classroom, so that I can go on teaching'. All adults in school should be trained in the legally correct and safe ways of touching pupils if they have to.

Ways of encouraging motivation and achievement

It is useful constantly to review approaches and strategies that succeed in helping vulnerable youngsters with TS to remain motivated.

- Encourage learning styles that involve more risk taking challenges for girls and more reflection for boys in Key Stages 1 and 2 to help undo any gender stereotyping they might have encountered.
- Negotiate with them targets for attainment that have as baselines pupils' own experiences, strengths and interests.
- Include curriculum and assessment materials that show individuals overcoming physical limitations and leading fulfilled lifestyles despite disabilities or disorders.
- Provide appropriate support and extra time to ensure that potential barriers to achievement such as restricted times for exams and tests are overcome.
- Use diverse assessment approaches including ICT to give pupils who have poor fine motor skills maximum opportunities to demonstrate their competencies.
- Provide extra time for pupils to catch up on missed work if their fine motor skills are under-developed and they write slowly or with difficulty.
- Arrange a safe spot inside or outside the classroom where pupils can withdraw if they need a short private break. This must be

pre-arranged and pupils and adults need to know precisely what the pupil can do to remove himself from a potentially stressful situation if is likely to escalate unfavourably for him.

- Encourage participation in every day events such as plays, visits and exploration of the environment to help strengthen pupils' willingness to venture out in the community with peers. This can help limit any inclinations to isolate themselves due to embarrassment about their tics or coprolalia.
- Spur on colleagues and parents/carers to encourage children to participate in sport, gymnastics, yoga or music making activities. Many youngsters with TS experience a reduction in their tics when they are participating in sport or other activity which they really enjoy.
- Teach essential rules for minimising risks of physical danger to themselves and others to encourage them to be more adventurous responsibly.

To make progress with improving primary behaviour some secondary inappropriate behaviour will need to be overlooked, but this must *not* include physical or verbal aggression and deliberate flouting of school rules.

1. *Physical aggression:* follow the school rules immediately and record fully if the incident is serious.
2. *Verbal aggression:* ask the pupil to stay behind after the lesson to discuss the incident privately and in a quieter environment and record if necessary. Children who have TS are at times rebuked for verbal outbursts, which may have been involuntary or which have been provoked by a subtle remark by a classmate. It is challenging for the adult to spot such a provocative act.
3. *Deliberate flouting of school rules:* defiance and refusal to start or carry out an activity when requested, wandering in and out of the cloakroom, deliberately disturbing other pupils, and throwing objects all need to be curtailed.

Helping pupils with TS/ADHD to re-focus their attention

Teachers need to develop particular skills to help pupils with TS/ADHD to re-focus their attention. It is preferable to catch the pupil's eye first, then a privately understood non-verbal signal may be used to remind the child what to do. Calling out the child's name should be restricted as far as possible as peers usually negatively label pupils whose names are often called out. The child may need to be reminded quietly of the school rule and what is expected of him. Tone of voice and body language can undo the positive message being conveyed, so keep these neutral. Give an enthusiastic straightforward comment about the child's ability to succeed.

Turn away from possible confrontation. Divert and distract a young child or a pupil who might become angry or confrontational. You should continue with teaching the group or individual and after a few minutes check that he has started his work or whether he may need a prompt or an explanation. Praising the other pupils who are demonstrating on-task behaviour can be particularly effective with younger children. Arrange for the child to sit near peers who conform appropriately and who do not provoke or stimulate inappropriate behaviour in others.

Poor readers benefit from visual clues so when writing instructions on the whiteboard, try using symbols instead of words. The pupil with ADHD/TS requires frequent variations in pace and change of task. Follow more routine work like handwriting with something more stimulating, such as a group discussion.

If a senior pupil is easily distracted by noises, consider letting him use a headset with music of his choice when he is working independently. His lack of concentration may be a side effect of, or drowsiness due to medication, and this should be reported to his parents and through them to his doctor.

Give-and-take can work wonders. Remember to keep in mind the child's individual targets, the benefits of allowing him some say in the curriculum and the importance of helping him at all times to sustain his self-esteem and positive relationships with others.

As pupils grow older, swearing which is done on purpose inevitably becomes an increasing problem for school staff. It is exacerbated for that minority of adolescent pupils with TS in whom coprolalia is present and who express involuntarily obscene or socially inappropriate syllables, words or phrases or repeat the words of others, sometimes in a loud explosive manner. Again, for that small minority of pupils with coprolalia extreme sensitivity is needed because, as Shimberg (1995) has noted, 'for those who cannot mask the words or substitute something more socially acceptable, coprolalia is the most disturbing verbal tic. Coprolalia causes trouble at school, causes workers to lose their jobs, and closes many doors on social utterances and peer support'.

Rewards please most pupils most of the time

It is surely every educator's desire that learners should find learning intrinsically so rewarding that they perform the desired behaviour without receiving any more reward than praise and self-satisfaction. This is an ideal worth pursuing, but in the interim there will be those pupils for whom rewards present requisite parts of behaviour modification programmes to improve pupils' motivation, self-esteem and behaviour.

Researchers who have studied closely the behaviour of pupils with TS have highlighted the effectiveness of reward systems (Shimberg 1995; Dornbush and Pruitt 1993; Bruun and Bruun 1994).

There are two elements to praise: what the child hears and the message that the child internalises. For example, if low marks are awarded for a piece of work, the pupil is more likely to remember this, regardless of any encouraging comments written alongside. If a pupil with TS has been asked to clear away and refuses, repeat the instruction. When he does acquiesce, don't necessarily praise him, but do provide explicit feedback: 'The table is tidy now, thank you, and ready for the next class'. If he acquiesces noisily, turn away. Focus on the primary behavioural goal and ignore the secondary annoying flounces, however maddening. Keep modelling good interpersonal skills and retain a warm relationship with him.

Be wary of over-doing the praise of older pupils with TS/ADHD for carrying out routine tasks, which they know they should and can easily do and for which their classmates are not praised.

In a classroom where some pupils have specific reward systems linked to their IEP targets, those rewards should also be available to everyone in the class for effort and achievement.

Case Study: Wesley

WESLEY is a shy, withdrawn pupil who has TS and he makes a huge effort constantly to manage his tics and impulsive behaviour. He gets overlooked because he is so quiet but when he is given a certificate – however brief – to take home, he does find it hugely motivating and his mother appreciates it greatly.

When feasible, all adults associated with the pupils with SEN should be involved in administering any rewards and should cooperate to move the pupil on from material affirmative tokens to intrinsic feelings of satisfaction. Strengthening the ability of pupils with TS/ADHD/OCD to value their own efforts, reflect on their progress and to give themselves praise, can bestow on them a gift for life.

It boosts a pupil's self-esteem and social skills if he can involve classmates in any reward time such as extra sessions on a computer. This allows him to practise his social skills and build up his social and academic skills while rewarding him for his effort.

Rewards should be motivating and spur achievement:

- Rewards or consequences given soon after the achievement are most beneficial.
- Allow praise or consequences to have an effect. Most reward systems fail because adults give up on them too soon.
- Change rewards frequently after establishing what most motivates the pupils.
- Point systems may be too abstract for pupils with ADHD/TS or very young pupils, so concentrate on giving reinforcers such as stars or certificates. Popular activities as rewards include: cleaning the board, setting the video recorder, helping younger children, delivering messages, being first in the dinner queue.
- Reward the pupil for initiating his own time-out rather than losing control in class.
- Avoid reward systems becoming mechanical or routine.

Do not overlook your own rewards. You are not an endless resource for others and deserve to give yourself some treats and time to unwind fully.

Using consequences to set boundaries

The most constructive approaches to sanctions: make a clear distinction between minor and more serious offences . . . [ensure they] are planned and not administered *ad hoc* . . . and respect pupils' dignity and self-esteem.
(OFSTED 1993)

Increasing the severity of punishment does not necessarily mean that the inappropriate behaviour will diminish and it is often the certainty of consequences that is more effective than the severity. Consequences need to teach the pupil something about the appropriate behaviour that is required to reduce the likelihood of transgressions being repeated, they should be fairly administered and should always be known to pupils in advance. When pupils make it difficult for others to learn or to feel safe then they can expect consequences to follow.

Turning theory into solutions

The motto of a Boeing 747 allegedly is 'If at first you don't succeed, fly, fly and fly again' (Loomans 1996). When backing children with TS/ADHD/OCD it is vital to show continuing faith in their abilities to succeed despite obstacles they may encounter in school. School staff and parents have found the following strategies effective when providing support.

Daydreaming

A pupil who seems to be inattentive or daydreaming may be repressing his tics.

Disclosing information about TS

There is a fine balance between providing information in such a way that will empower peers to be compassionate and supportive and talking about it in ways that focus on the disorder rather than on the whole individual.

- Seek the pupil's and parents' guidance and permission about disclosing to his classmates the nature of TS and associated behaviours that affect his education.
- Explore the potential of allowing a pupil to record his experiences and feelings onto a video recorder and then play the cassette to his classmates according to his preferred presence or his absence. Teenagers who have done this have encountered significant improvements in peer understanding and support.

Homework

Homework causes huge strain in many households and where a pupil's TS symptoms already cause extra stress homework can compound this. Neurologically impaired pupils usually also experience deterioration in attention and concentration as the day and term progress. Teachers may need to adjust their expectations.

- Enlist parents' support in ensuring that pupils have and use their homework diaries.
- Peers with good language skills can take turns to copy down homework that is particularly detailed into a small notebook with carbon sheets. The pupil with TS takes the book and the other pupil staples the sheets into his notebook.
- Ask parents to keep a supply of necessary materials and equipment such as pens, paper, rulers in one place at home and to sign completed homework.

Maths

Many youngsters with TS find written maths very complex to grasp even though they might be capable of applying it in every day life, e.g. adding cricket scores quickly. Rote learning of mathematical facts can be difficult for pupils who have TS/ADHD as this requires sutained focus on something that may not interest them, concentration and sequential memorising, all of which present them with obstacles to learning.

- Encourage use of different sensory materials and number charts before requesting pupils to recall abstract concepts.
- Teach pupils to use cognitive and visual clues to recall calculation sequences.
- Provide paper with adequate spacings to work out problems and align digits.
- Try and provide prepared copies of problems to limit need for copying down.
- Reduce the number of sums or problems to be completed, but expect accuracy.
- Be sensitive about involving the pupil in class mental maths activities or timed tests.
- Allow the use of calculators with large keys or extra access to computer games or programmes, but don't let this mask lack of mastery of essential facts and skills.
- Games and CD-Rom activities are highly motivating and can enhance learning.

Perfectionism

Pupils who have TS/OCD may work inordinately slowly if they are excessive about perfectionism and this may be hard to spot as individuals understandably might try to conceal this trait. They may become irritated when asked to switch activities if they feel they have not finished their task properly.

- Break work down into shorter segments. Give pupils gentle reminders when the end of a session is near. Young children can use egg timers as prompts.

Reading

Tics such as head shaking or involuntary eye movements may cause a child to lose his place when reading and inevitably make the task more burdensome.

- Arrange extra one-to-one support where possible, encourage him to use a bookmark or ruler to keep his place as he reads, let him use a highlighter to mark important passages.
- Allow extra access to computer language programmes or books on disk.

Restlessness

Pupils who have TS/ADHD are usually very restless, are easily distracted, and may find sitting still and listening, waiting their turns and not calling out inappropriately extremely stressful.

- Pre-arrange with them how they can take short breaks to move around, have a drink, go to the toilet, put their heads down.

Rules

In lessons on Citizenship negotiate and establish with the class clear rules.

- Display the rules at eye level in the front of the room. All pupils needs to be clear about what they gain if they keep the rules and what they lose if they don't.

School phobias and refusals

For some pupils with TS the school environment may be the place where they face the most formidable hurdles leading them to begin to avoid or refuse to attend school.

- Cooperate with parents, health agencies and LEA advisory services to help the pupil take small steps to returning to school full time.

Self-organisation

Organising their time and belongings is a burden for many pupils.

- Keep requests as simple and as specific as possible.
- Teach prioritisation, realistic goal setting and self-organisation skills.
- Set generous but specific time limits for tidying away equipment.
- Ask parents/carers to let the child prepare for school at night before he goes to bed.

Specific learning difficulties

There is a high incidence of learning disabilities such as poor memory skills and visual-motor integration problems associated with TS (Bruun and Bruun 1994) which can cause pupils to experience extra frustration in school. These need to be urgently addressed through school-based identification and support arrangements and through collaboration with other professionals and the LEA's advisory service.

Tests

Where necessary allow tests to be taken in a separate room with extended timing and possible use of ICT.

Tiredness

Pupils with TS/ADHD/OCD may often appear tired in school because they frequently experience difficulty going to sleep and stay up late to read, watch television or engage in other activities; they may take medication that makes them drowsy and may have rituals they repeat frequently leaving them very fatigued.

- Give instructions more slowly and try to reinforce them in diverse ways.

Writing

A pupil's visual-motor difficulties can delay completion and impair presentation of work. If he appears lazy, it may be due to the huge effort he has to make to finish a task. To write effectively he has to integrate may cognitive skills, concentrate, use fine motor skills successfully and self-monitor. He may make spelling and punctuation errors despite knowing the rules, due to lack of practice because of his considerable resistance to write. Hand and arm tics may make the child produce irregular, shaky letters or cause him to press too hard on the paper pushing right through it.

- Consider letting the pupil choose to print instead of doing cursive writing.
- Try and provide copies of teacher's notes or lesson plans to reduce problems encountered when copying down.
- Learning aids such as electronic notebooks, word processors, calculators and sometimes tape recorders can be tried for routine assignments as well as for special projects or reports.
- Arrange oral tests instead of some written tests occasionally.
- Pupils with OCD may feel compelled to write and re-write, sometimes erasing so hard that they make holes in the paper. An occupational therapist can advise on improving pencil grips and using devices to improve grip.
- Shorten the expected length of the writing task to meet the child's present ability and increase it as he progresses. Bear in mind, however, that low expectations may be as demotivating as expectations that are too high.

Chapter 9

Ensuring Inclusion is a Process and not a State

Whether mainstream education systems can be designed and operated to meet the full diversity of individual needs without some differentiation or internal organisation for a minority, is a continuing issue. (Norwich 1999)

The 1989 Children Act introduced radical legal changes relating to the care and education of children and made it legally obligatory to consult pupils about their SEN plans if their views can be ascertained (Galloway *et al.* 1994; Government 1989). The United Nations Convention on the Rights of the Child further underpins such prerogatives. In the UK such provision is also covered in the *Code of Practice on the Identification and Assessment of Special Educational Needs* (DFE 1994) – known usually as the 'Code' or 'CoP'. Although not legally binding, schools are expected to take cognisance of it and are encouraged to make every effort to identify the ascertainable views and wishes of youngsters as: 'Young people are more likely to respond positively to intervention programmes if they fully understand the rationale for their involvement and if they are given some powerful responsibility for their own progress' (DFE 1994).

Roller (1998) has shown how well placed educators are to undertake and support school initiatives to extend these rights to all children. Having analysed pupil's views on the curriculum, she concluded that not only do many pupils wish to be consulted but they also have constructive insights and comments to offer. When pupils are consulted they are more willing to take greater responsibility for their learning and also to help others through various befriending, buddy and mentoring systems. All of these are linked, as Roller records with enhancement of pupil motivation, perception of control, confidence and empowerment.

We know how much pupils with TS welcome being consulted on any strategies to sustain their progress. Allowing all pupils to play active parts in these activities can be incorporated into PSHE and Citizenship lessons. The new frameworks for PSHE and Citizenship

Accommodating the pupil's views in the curriculum

give schools for the first time explicit directions for continuing to engage directly in helping pupils address their personal and social needs. The non-statutory framework for PSHE and Citizenship at Key Stages (KS) 1 and 2 and for PSHE at KS 3 and 4 are due to be implemented by September 2000. A new foundation subject in Citizenship for KS 3 and 4 will become statutory from August 2002 (DfEE and QCA 1999).

Case Study: Nathan

NATHAN, a Y6 pupil who has TS, was finding it extremely stressful to go out at playtimes and lunch breaks, as often he would end up arguing or fighting with others. Repeatedly he would be sent in to see the head teacher and despite many discussions and attempts by staff to modify his IEP and give him adequate support, he continued to experience difficulties outside the classroom. One Monday morning he brought in from home a new CD-Rom which had maths games on it and asked his teacher if he could stay in at playtime and work on it. His teacher agreed provided he chose a classmate to stay in with him. So he did and they worked harmoniously. His partner asked if they could stay in at lunch and finish a game. His teacher negotiated with them that they could after going outside for ten minutes to get some fresh air. This pattern continued with Nathan choosing different classmates. As a result of this enjoyable, stress-free time with him, his classmates experienced a side of him they had previously not known. There was distinct improvement in Nathan's enjoyment of school and after about six weeks he happily began to spend more time outside with his classmates.

Case Study: Sandra

SANDRA, a Y8 pupil, has only recently been diagnosed as having TS. She has had many problems with the curriculum and has fallen behind her classmates dramatically due to what it seemed were learning difficulties. As a result she became increasingly disaffected, started truanting and became more and more verbally aggressive. Last year she changed school and it was at the suggestion of that school's psychologist that her parents took her to their new GP to discuss her continuing difficulties. He diagnosed TS and made arrangements for her to have regular occupational therapy (OT) sessions after school. The results were stunning. The occupational therapist helped Sandra improve her fine motor skills by giving her a special handle on her pencil, teaching her to hold it differently and by playing visual-motor games with her, such as drawing mazes and completing Celtic patterns, and teaching her to do simple embroidery. These improvements gave her the self-confidence at school to explain to the form tutor how she had struggled with fine motor skills and how embarrassing this had been. She asked him if she could have extra time to improve her word processing skills and follow a staged language development computer programme. He organised this, she was able to work independently and her tics decreased. She loved this and made rapid progress, which she found highly motivating, allowing her not only to make strides academically but also to gain that all important hike in credibility in the eyes of her classmates. Her aggressive behaviour diminished, her truanting dwindled and she started making real friendships for the first time at school.

These successes were the outcomes of teachers listening to Nathan's and Sandra's own requests for help, and modifying the curriculum slightly for them. Problem behaviour is often an expression of deep anxiety, frustration and powerlessness by a pupil. Support programmes like these for Nathan and Sandra that address these strong feelings can be very rewarding for adults and children alike.

When a teacher is receptive to involving pupils more directly, he or she can gain greater insights into making arrangements for pupils with TS that they find motivating and relevant and that need not involve staff in any extra duties. Much does depend, however, on the pupil's age, knowledge and understanding of what such options might represent. Pupils such as Nathan and Sandra are too often on the receiving end of pastoral attention in schools and too seldom are invited to give pastoral support to others. For a pupil with TS to be a mentor or a buddy can be exceptionally motivating as too frequently they are viewed as sufferers and victims, and their insights into how they could befriend others with disorders or disabilities are overlooked.

Empathising with pupils

For some youngsters with TS adolescence can be a depressing and lonely time if they are not in a school environment that fosters their self-esteem and teaches them how to make and sustain friendships. Being listened to by adults can help them overcome worries. It gives them that extra security of knowing they have someone to turn to when stuck and that they will be understood and empowered to make decisions for themselves.

- Organise a meeting where there is privacy but leave the door open for your mutual safety.
- If you are worried about a private meeting being misconstrued, think of inviting a colleague to be present in the room, but obtain the pupil's prior agreement.
- Do not sit opposite the pupil but at an angle, as it is less confrontational, and agree the length of time of the meeting.
- Introduce the topic by talking about areas of progress and achievement before leading into areas of concern.
- Assure the pupil of confidentiality up to a point, i.e. you are not going to gossip about shared information, but if anyone's safety or health is at risk, you have a responsibility to report this – and the pupil needs to be informed of that at the outset.
- Be friendly but do not encourage the pupil to become over-dependent on you.
- Allow for silence as it can provide a peaceful space for the pupil or you to reflect on what is being discussed.
- Think ahead of what your responses might be and be prepared for the possibility of emotional outbursts: tears, denials, and threats. If you are considering behavioural issues, help the pupil to role model or mirror some alternative responses.
- Search jointly for a solution for whatever is bothering the pupil and clarify what will be the options or next steps. If needed, agree a time for another meeting.
- End on an upbeat note. Always thank the pupil for talking and listening to you.

Setting reasonable goals

Records of achievement (ROAs) and IEPs have proved to be effective ways of helping many pupils with SEN including TS to work in partnership with staff to construct programmes for focus and assessment records. Schedules broken down into small steps are usually more motivating and easier to achieve.

Personal ROA or IEP goals for pupils with TS/ADHD are:

- being able to listen more often to others' views when working in pairs or groups
- improving hand–eye coordination when copying from the board
- making appropriate responses when behavioural goals are met or remain unmet
- responding appropriately to triggers for angry feelings and managing own time-out arrangements
- gradually following a more complex sequence of instructions
- beginning to offer to read aloud in class
- completing increasing amounts of homework.

Extra support for pupils with Tourette Syndrome

If a teacher becomes aware of a child's unusual behavioural patterns or there are changes in a pupil's behaviour, she is expected to make informal notes and to share her initial concerns with her colleagues and the child's parents.

The 1993 Education Act and the Code which it spawned are crucial documents in understanding the responsibilities and duties of LEAs, schools, parents, health and social services and others regarding all children who have TS. From 1 September 1994 it has been a requirement that all who work with children with SEN must have regard to this Code, although it is not prescribed in the Code what should be done in individual cases.

These school-based approaches to identifying and meeting pupils' SEN are enabled by the 1981 Education Act, which gave Local Education Authorities (LEAs) extensive autonomy to decide how to provide for children with SEN. (Galloway *et al.* 1994). The principles enshrined in the 1993 Act and Code are extensions of the duties and principles which were set out in the 1981 Act to ensure that children with SEN are integrated with their peers for as much of the time as is 'reasonably practicable'.

The Education Act 1981 is one of the important landmarks of education legislation this century, officially moving practice away from labelling towards more diagnosis and understanding of impairment and identifying areas of strength before planning intervention. It enshrines the rights of parents to be involved in the process of assessment and decision making as partners and allows pupils with SEN to be educated alongside their peers in ordinary schools to the maximum extent possible.

Since 1981 successive government reports have emphasised commitment to the general principle of inclusion and the responsibilities of schools to address the needs of all their pupils. Parents' worries over whether their children who have TS should be educated in mainstream or special schools have not yet been satisfied by these developments. In a publication from the National Association for Special Educational Needs (NASEN 1999) the two sides of the inclusion debate are clearly stated: Some parents, professionals and some disabled people themselves, argue that children deprived of mainstream access are being denied a basic human right to be educated alongside their peers. Others point out that SEN children in mainstream school are not having their needs met, as they require an appropriate curriculum, resources and positive staff attitudes and skills to ensure meaningful inclusion.

Collaboration with parents

It is explained in the Code that LEAs have a duty to educate children in mainstream schools, as long as: the child's needs can be properly met; there is no adverse effect on the education of the other children; resources are used effectively; and parents agree. Where provision for pupils with TS is seen as a whole-school matter to be consistently synchronised in partnership with parents and health officials, pupils progress best.

Successful inclusion is a process not a state, and involves far more than suitability of placements. Parents are crucial factors in the success of a school's support programmes and their knowledge, views and experience are vital. Much can depend on parents' choice of educational placement, whether their child is accepted there and subsequently how much support they can give their child to help deal with those trials that schooling offers even the most confident child.

Making schools truly inclusive

It is the teachers' responsibility to ensure that all pupils progress and achieve and it is the duty of the head teacher and governing body to ensure this. They have overall responsibility for overseeing the school's general policy and procedures for pupils with SEN and establishing the correct staffing and funding arrangements. All mainstream schools are expected to follow a five staged approach to support children with SEN and to appoint a designated teacher as Special Educational Needs Coordinator (SENCO), to be responsible for coordinating such provision (DFE 1994).

Stage One
The class or form teacher, or any other adult, identifies concerns, registers details, monitors findings and is expected to discuss them with the pupil and his/her parents. The class teacher needs to inform colleagues, particularly the school's SENCO and the focus here is on collating information, increasing differentiation within the pupil's normal classroom situation and reviewing developments. The head teacher may be informed. For pupils with TS, as with all SEN, there is a continuum of needs and of provision, and diverse support arrangements are needed in response.

Stage Two

If the difficulties persist, an IEP detailing the problems and available support is drawn up and specialist advice is sought from members of the health services or the LEA's educational psychology or advisory services. The SENCO takes responsibility for coordinating provision of support, but the teachers remain responsible for teaching the pupil. An IEP should, where possible, incorporate the views of pupils, parents and other involved adults. The head teacher needs to be informed. Advice obtained from other agencies should be implemented. When the IEP is reviewed, if it is decided that the pupil needs extra support in the classroom, the decision may be taken to move the child on to Stage Three.

Stage Three

The SENCO continues to take the lead role here while cooperating with the pupil's teachers, ensuring pupil and parents are consulted, keeping the head teacher informed and liaising with other agencies. If concerns about a child's needs have continued and school interventions have not been sufficient to meet these needs satisfactorily, an educational psychologist will be asked to assess the child and then to advise whether a further assessment for a 'statement' of special educational needs is required. If the educational psychologist decides that a pupil has serious learning and behavioural difficulties and his needs cannot reasonably be met within resources normally available to mainstream schools locally, the educational psychologist can recommend that a statutory assessment be undertaken.

Stage Four

The needs of children with TS can be met effectively under these school-based stages without the LEA's involvement. In a minority of cases, however, the LEA will make a statutory assessment of a pupil's SEN. The educational psychologist is a key figure here assessing the needs of the pupil, advising the school on ways of modifying support, providing training if requested and liaising with parents. The educational psychologist submits to the LEA an assessment of a pupil's strengths and weaknesses if a request has been made to the LEA for a statement to be compiled by parents, the child's school or another agency such as social services. If parents make the request, the LEA must react quickly and can only refuse if it has already decided a statement is unnecessary, or the child has already been formally assessed over the previous six months. Before an educational psychologist can assess a child, parental permission must be obtained.

Stage Five

The main circumstance for issuing a statement arises when the pupil's school cannot reasonably meet her SEN out of its normal budget. A statement sets out a child's educational and other needs, the educational objectives to be achieved, the provision to be made and the monitoring and review arrangements.

Children from as young as two years can be given a statement, which is a legally binding document setting out how these needs will be met. Statutory assessment does not always lead to a statement if the LEA decides that the school can meet a pupil's needs without one. When a statement is first issued and then subsequently at annual reviews, parents have the right to say which school they prefer their child to attend and the LEA must agree, subject to certain conditions. When a maintained school is named on a child's statement, that school must accept the child. These assessments and statements have to be written in prescribed time limits.

Although over recent years public awareness and knowledge about TS has substantially increased, many school staff members still have insufficient information about effectively supporting a pupil with TS. There is a clear need for further training being made available to them to ensure children with TS obtain equal opportunities for a broad and balanced education as secured under the 1988 Education Reform Act and re-affirmed in the new National Curriculum.

Tourette Syndrome in Public Life and in Literature

Well known people with Tourette Syndrome

Not many well known people have been suggested to have TS. One of the most convincing suggestions was that Dr Samuel Johnson had TS (McHenry 1967; Murray 1979). He made many motor tics and movements and had curious vocal tics such as whistling and the sound of a whale exhaling. He also had echolalia (copying what other people say), and SIB in that he would cut his nails too deep until they bled. He was a religious man and did not have coprolalia, but had the curious vocal tic of uttering bits of the Lord's Prayer into an otherwise normal conversation.

There have also been suggestions (Simkin 1992) that Wolfgang Amadeus Mozart had TS. These suggestions arose as Mozart indulged in scatalogical (obscene) writings in his very prolific letters. In our opinion, however, Mozart had no typical motor nor vocal tics, no ADHD, no OCB/D and no relevant family history. The obscenities in his letters were written on purpose and moreover must be taken in context.

It has also been convincingly speculated that Tolstoy's brother, Dmitri, had TS. His story was portrayed in the character Nicolai Levin in the classic text *Anna Karenina* (Hurst and Hurst 1994).

Julius Wechter (the marimba player of the group known in the 1960s as Herb Alpert's Tijuana Brass) also has TS (Robertson and Baron-Cohen 1998).

Jim Eisenreich, a famous American major league baseball player, has TS. He first had symptoms such as rapid eye blinking at the age of six years which led to a diagnosis of hyperactivity; he was told he would 'grow out of it'. Seventeen years elapsed before he had a correct diagnosis. He has played for the Minnesota Twins, Kansas City Royals, Philadelphia Phillies and the Los Angeles Dodgers. He established a Foundation for TS children in 1996, and is active in public awareness and fundraising efforts for the American TS Association (Shimberg 1995).

A well known Canadian surgeon who is also an aeroplane pilot with a private licence, Dr Mort Doran, has TS. He only learned of his disorder when he was 36 years old. He heard a neurologist on the radio discussing TS, personally identified with the symptoms – and went on to learn that he had TS and OCD. For a full account of his enlightening story the reader is referred to Shimberg (1995).

Peter Hollenbeck, an afflicted neuroscientist, is an associate professor in the Department of Biological Sciences at Purdue University in West Lafayette, Indiana, USA. He gives an excellent and moving account of having TS, and how having it diagnosed and finally treated really did change his life (Hollenbeck 1999).

Tourette Syndrome in popular literature

Dr Oliver Sacks was probably the first to bring the world of TS into popular literature, with chapters in two of his books being devoted to individuals with TS (Witty Ticcy Ray in *The Man Who Mistook his Wife for a Hat* 1987; A Surgeon's Life in *An Anthropologist on Mars* 1995).

More recent novels in the popular literature in which people with TS play important roles include Sue Grafton's book *H is for Homicide* (Grafton 1992) in which a key character has TS, but also quite clearly has an acknowledged antisocial/psychopathic personality disorder.

On the other hand, in *Motherless Brooklyn* (Lethem 2000), the hero Lionel Essrog has severe TS, the symptoms of which are very well described. Lionel comes across as a personable and attractive individual, and for anyone interested in TS, it is a must for reading.

Paul Skoglund is the hero of Daniel Hecht's (1998) book, *Skull Session*. Paul also has TS and, because of it, he has not held down a job for some time. The book involves the intrigues of Janet (Paul's ex wife, who is trying to get custody of their son) as well as the horrors discovered when Paul helps a wealthy aunt repair her hunting lodge.

Tourette Syndrome Fact Sheet

THE NATIONAL HOSPITAL FOR NEUROLOGY
AND NEUROSURGEY
Queen Square, London WC1N 3BG
Telephone: 0171 837 3611
Fax: 0171 829 8720

GILLES DE LA TOURETTE'S SYNDROME

(Tourette's Syndrome: TS)

FACT SHEET

Professor Mary M Robertson

<u>Criteria</u>	American Psychiatric Association (DSM-IV) 1994	
	World Health Organisation (ICD-10) 1992	
<u>Essential Features</u>	Multiple motor tics (twitches):	number =
	One or more vocal tics (noises):	number =

COPROLALIA (inappropriate involuntary swearing tic)

TS Clinics	30%	
General population	2-4%	
Overall	10%	
Patient:		YES/NO

COPROPRAXIA (inappropriate involuntary V sign tic)

TS Clinics	20%	
Patient:		YES/NO

ECHOLALIA (copying what others say):   YES/NO

ECHOPRAXIA (copying what others do):   YES/NO

PALILALIA (repeating one's own words):   YES/NO

PALIPRAXIA (repeating one's own actions):   YES/NO

Obsessive compulsive behaviours (OCB):   YES/NO

Self-injurious behaviours (SIB):   YES/NO

Depression: YES/NO

The University College London Hospitals

University College London Hospitals is an NHS Trust incorporating The Eastman Dental Hospital, The Hospital for Tropical Diseases, The Middlesex Hospital, The National Hospital for Neurology & Neurosurgery, The United Elizabeth Garrett Anderson Hospital and Hospital for Women, Soho, and University College Hospital.

TS Fact Sheet (cont'd)

Depression Scales: BIRLESON ....
                                  KOVACS ....
                                  BECK ....

Attention Deficit Hyperactivity Disorder (ADHD):   YES/NO

Oppositional Defiant Disorder (ODD):   YES/NO

Conduct Disorder (CD):   YES/NO

Cause

a)   Genetic   Autosomal dominant

                      TS/OCB

                      Heterogeneity - different genes in different families

b)   Perinatal complications

c)   Biochemical - dopamine)
)   in basal ganglia
                      seratonin)

SEVERITY

a)   Yale Global Tic Severity Rating Scale   ....%

b)   Diagnostic Confidence Index   ....%

c)   MOVES   ....%

Conclusion

Severity = mild / moderate / severe

TS Fact Sheet (cont'd)

MEDICATION	<u>Neuroleptics</u>	Sulpiride
		Haloperidol
		Pimozide
		Risperidone
	<u>Clonidine</u>	
	<u>SSRI's new</u>	Fluoxetine
		Fluvoxamine
		Paroxetine
		Sertraline
		Citalopram
	<u>old</u>	Clomipramine
	<u>Stimulants</u>	Methyl Phenidate (Ritalin)
		Dextroamphetamine
	<u>Others</u>	

<u>NB</u>

- No relationship to lifespan
- No relationship to psychosis ('madness')
- Often improves with age
- Most TS individuals in the community are mild
- UK Tourette Syndrome Association - Q&A Leaflet

Appendix C

Useful Addresses and Contact Numbers

ADD Information Services Ms Andrea Bilbow, PO Box 340, Edgware, Middlesex, HA8 9HL. Tel: 020 8906 9068. Fax: 020 8959 0727. Website: www.addiss.co.uk email: info@addiss.co.uk

ADD-ADHD Family Support Group 1a High Street, Dilton Marsh, Westbury, Wilts, BA13 4DL. Tel: 01373 826045.

Hyperactive Children's Support Group Mrs Sally Bunday, 71 Whyke Lane, Chichester, West Sussex, PO9 2LD. Tel: 01903 725 182. Fax: 01903 734 726.

Obsessive Action PO Box 6097, London, W2 1WZ.

OC Foundation (Inc) PO Box 9573, New Haven, CT 06535, USA. email:infor@ocfoundation.org

OCD International Website http://www.ocdresource.com

Tourette Syndrome (UK) Association 1st Floor Offices, Old Bank Chambers, London Road, Crowborough, East Sussex, TN6 2TT. Tel: 01892 669151. Fax: 01892 663 649. email:TSA_UK@compuserv.com

Tourette Syndrome Association (Inc) 42–40 Bell Boulevard, Bayside, NY 11631-2820, USA. Tel (718) 224 2999. Fax (718) 279 9596. email: tourette@ix.netcom.com Website: http://tsa.mgh.harvard.edu/

References

Abuzzahab, F. E. and Anderson, F. O. (1973) Gilles de la Tourette's syndrome. *Minnesota Medicine*, **56**, 492–6.

American Psychiatric Association (1980) *Diagnostic and Statistical Manual of Mental Disorders (3rd edition), (DSM 111)*. Washington DC: American Psychiatric Association.

American Psychiatric Association (1987) *Diagnostic and Statistical Manual of Mental Disorders (3rd edition revised), (DSM-III-R)*. Washington DC: American Psychiatric Association.

American Psychiatric Association (1994) *Diagnostic and Statistical Manual of Mental disorders (4th edition), (DSM-IV)*. Washington DC: American Psychiatric Association.

Apter, A. *et al.* (1993) 'An epidemiological study of Gilles de la Tourette's syndrome in Israel' *Archives of General Psychiatry* **50**, 734–8.

Barkley, R. A. *et al.* (2000) 'Multi-method psycho-educational intervention for preschool children with disruptive behavior: preliminary results at post-treatment' *Journal of Child Psychology and Psychaitry* **41**(3), 319–332.

Baron-Cohen, S. and Bolton, P. (1993) *Autism: The Facts*. Oxford: Oxford University Press.

Baron-Cohen, S. *et al.* (1999a) The prevalence of Gilles de la Tourette's syndrome in children and adolescents with autism. *Journal of Child Psychology and Psychiatry*, **40**(2), 213–18.

Baron-Cohen, S. *et al.* (1999b) The prevalence of Gilles de la Tourette syndrome in children and adolescents with autism: a large scale study. *Psychological Medicine*, **29**, 1115–59.

Berkson, J. (1946) Limitations of the application of fourfold table analysis to hospital data. *Biometrics*, **2**, 47–51.

Bliss, J. (1980) Sensory experiences of Gilles de la Tourette Syndrome. *Archives of General Psychiatry*, **37**, 1343–7.

Bruun, R. D. (1984) Gilles de la Tourette's syndrome: an overview of clinical experience. *Journal of the American Academy of Child and Adolescent Psychiatry*, **23**, 126–33.

Bruun, R. D. (1988) Subtle and underrecognized side effects of neuroleptic treatment in children with Tourette's disorder. *American Journal of Psychiatry*, **145**, 621–4.

Bruun, R. D. and Bruun, B. (1994) *A Mind of its Own*. New York: Oxford University Press.

Budman, C. L, *et al.* (1998) Rage attacks in children and adolescents with Tourette's disorder: a pilot study. *Journal of Clinical Psychiatry,* **59**(11), 576–80.

Burd, L. and Kerbeshian, J. (1992) 'Educational Management of Children with Tourette Syndrome', *Advances in Neurology,* **58,** 311–17.

Carter, A. S. *et al.* (2000) Social and emotional adjustment in children affected with Gilles de la Tourette's syndrome: associations with ADHD and family functioning. *Journal of Child Psychology and Psychiatry* **41**(2), 215–23.

Channon, S. *et al.* (1992) 'Attention deficits in the Gilles de la Tourette Syndrome', *Neuropsychiatry, Neurospyschology and Behavioural Neurology* **5**(3), 170–7.

Cohen, D. J. *et al.* (1988) *Tourette's Syndrome & Tic Disorders.* New York: John Wiley & Sons.

Cohen, A. J. Leckman, J. F. (1992) Sensory phenomena associated with Gilles de la Tourette Syndrome. *Journal of Clinical Psychiatry,* **53**, 319–23.

Cohen, D. J. *et al.* (1992) Tourette's syndrome: A model developmental neuropsychiatric disorder. In Chiland, C. Young and J. G. (eds.) *New Approaches to Mental health from Birth to Adolescence* 121–52. New Haven, CT: Yale University Press.

Comings, D. E. *et al.* (1990) An epidemiologic study of Tourette's syndrome in a single school district. *Journal of Clinical Psychiatry,* **51**, 563–9.

Cooper, P. and Ideus, K. (1996) *Attention Deficit Hyperactivity Disorder: A practical guide for teachers.* London: David Fulton Publishers.

Costello, E. J. *et al.* (1996) The Great Smoky Mountains Study of Youth. Goals, design, methods, and the prevalence of DSM-111-R Disorders. *Archives of General Psychiatry,* **53**, 1129–36.

Covey, S. R. (1990) *The 7 Habits of Highly Effective People.* New York: Simon & Schuster.

Cumine, V. *et al.* (1998) *Asperger Syndrome: A practical guide for teachers.* London: David Fulton Publishers.

De Groot, C. M. *et al.* (1995) Clinical predictors of psychopathology in children and adolescents with Tourette Syndrome. *Journal of Psychiatric Research,* **29**(1), 59–70.

DFE (1994) *Code of Practice on the Identification and Assessment of Special Educational Needs.* London: HMSO.

DFE (1994a) *Pupil Behaviour and Discipline,* Circular 8/94. London: DFE.

DfEE (1997) *Starting with Quality.* London: HMSO.

DfEE (1999) *Social Inclusion: Pupil Support,* Circular 10/99. London: DfEE.

DfEE and QCA (1999*) The National Curriculum.* London: HMSO.

Dornbush, M. P. and Pruitt, S. K. (1993) *Teaching the Tiger.* Duarte, CA: Hope Press.

Eapen, V. *et al.* (1993) Evidence for autosomal dominant transmission in Gilles de la Tourette syndrome – United Kingdom cohort. *British Journal of Psychiatry,* **162**, 593–6.

Eapen, V. *et al.* (1997) Gilles de la Tourette's syndrome in special education schools: a United Kingdom study. *Journal of Neurology,* **244**, 378–82.

Eapen, V. and Robertson, M. M. (2000) 'Co-morbid obsessive compulsive disorder and Tourette Syndrome: therapeutic interventions', *CNS Drugs* **13**(3), 173–83.

Erenberg, G. (1999) The clinical neurology of Tourette Syndrome, *CNS Spectrums,* **4**(2), 36–53.

Erenberg, G. *et al.* (1986) Tourette syndrome: An analysis of 200 pediatric and adolescent cases. *Cleveland Clinic Quarterly,* **53**,127–31

Fallon, T. and Scwab-Stone (1992) Methodology of Epidemiological Studies of Tic Disorders and Comorbid Psychopathology. *Advances in Neurology*, **58**, 43–53.

Faupel, A. *et al.* (1998) *Anger Management*. London: David Fulton Publishers.

Ferrari, M. *et al.* (1984) 'Children with Tourette Syndrome: results of psychological tests given prior to drug treatment', *Developmental and Behavioural Pediatrics* **5**, 116–19.

Finegold, I. (1985) Allergy and Tourette's Syndrome. *Annals of Allergy*, **55**, 119–21.

Fowler, R. (1996) *The Unwelcome Companion; An insider's view of Tourette Syndrome*. Athens, GA: Silver Run Publications.

Freeman, R. D. (1997) Attention deficit hyperactivity disorder in the presence of Tourette Syndrome. *Neurologic Clinics*, **15**(2), 411–20.

Freeman, R. D. *et al.* (2000) An international perspective on Tourette Syndrome: selected findings from 3,500 cases in 22 countries. *Developmental Medicine and Child Neurology* (in press).

Gaffney, G. R. *et al.* (1994) The MOVES: A self-rating scale for Tourette's Syndrome. *Journal of Child and Adolescent Psychopharmacology*, **4**(4), 269–80.

Galloway, D. *et al.* (1994) *The Assessment of Special Educational Needs*. Harlow: Longman.

Gilles de la Tourette, G. (1885) Etude sur une affection nerveuse caractérisée par de l'incoordination motrice accompagnee d'echolalie et de coprolalie. *Archives of Neurology*, **9**,19–42, 158–200.

Goetz, C. G. *et al.* (1987) A rating scale for Gilles de la Tourette's syndrome: description, reliability and validity data. *Neurology*, **37**, 1542–44.

Golden, G. S. and Greenhill, L. (1981) Tourette syndrome in mentally retarded children. *Mental Retardation*, **19**, 17.

Golden, G. S. and Hood, O. J. (1982) Tics and tremors. *Pediatric Clinics of North America*, **29**, 95–103.

Golden, G. S. (1984) Psychologic and and neuropsychologic aspects of Tourette's syndrome. *Neurologic Clinics*, **21**, 91–102.

Goleman, D. (1996) *Emotional Intelligence*. London: Bloomsbury Publishing.

Government publication (1989) *The Children Act Chapter 41*. London: HMSO.

Grafton, S. (1992) *H is for Homicide*. London: Pan Books (Macmillan General Books).

Hagin, R. A. *et al.* (1982) Effects of Tourette Syndrome on Learning. In Friedhoff, A. J. and Chase, T. N. (eds) *Gilles de la Tourette Syndrome*, 323–8. New York: Raven Press.

Hansen, C. R. (1992) What is Tourette Syndrome?, in Haerle, T. (ed.) *Children with Tourette Syndrome*, 1–25. Rockville: Woodbine House.

Haerle, T. (1992) (ed) *Children with Tourette Syndrome*. Rockville: Woodbine House.

Hecht, D. (1998) *Skull Session*. London: Pan Books (Macmillan General Books).

Hennessy, E. (1999) Children as service evaluators. *Child Psychology and Psychaitry Review*, **4**(4), 153–61.

Hollenbeck, P. (1999) 'How life imitates Tourette Syndrome: reflections of an afflicted neuroscientist', *CNS Spectrums* **4**(2), 22–3.

Holman, H. and Lorig, K. (2000) Patients as partners in managing chronic disease. *British Medical Journal*, **320**, 526–7.

Hurst, M. J. and Hurst, D. L. (1994) Tolstoy's description of Tourette syndrome in Anna Karenina. *Journal of Child Neurology*, **94**, 366–7.

Itard, J. M. G. (1825) Mémoire sur quelques fonctions involontaires des appareils de la locomotion de la prehension et de la voix. *Archives of General Medicine*, **8**, 365–407.

Kaplan, M. (1992) Daily life with your child, in Haerle, T. (ed.) *Children with*

Tourette Syndrome, 71–112. Rockville: Woodbine House.

Katona, C. and Robertson, M. (2000) *Psychiatry at a Glance* (2nd edition). Oxford: Blackwell Science.

King, R. A. *et al.* (1999) Psychosocial and behavioral treatments. In Leckman, J. F. Cohen, D. J. (eds) 338–59. *Tourette's Syndrome, Tics, Obsessions Compulsions.* New York: John Wiley & Sons Inc.

Kurlan, R. *et al.* (1994) Tourette's syndrome in a special education population: a pilot study involving a single school district. *Neurology,* 699–702.

Kurlan, R. *et al.* (1996) Non-obscene complex socially inappropriate behavior in Tourette's syndrome. *Journal of Neuropsychiatry and Clinical Neurosciences,* **8**, 311–17.

Kushner, H. I. (1999) *A Cursing Brain? The histories of Tourette Syndrome.* Cambridge (MA): Harvard University Press.

Leckman, J. F. *et al.* (1989) The Yale Global Tic Severity Scale. *Journal of the American Academy of Child and Adolescent Psychiatry,* **28**, 566–73.

Leckman, J. F. (1993) Premonitory urges in Tourette's syndrome. *American Journal of Psychiatry,* **150**, 98–102.

Leckman, J. F. *et al.* (1998) Course of tic severity in Tourette Syndrome: the first two decades. *Pediatrics,* **102**(1), 14–19.

Leckman, J. F. and Cohen, D. J. (1999) Beyond the Diagnosis – Darwinian Perspectives on Pathways to successful adaptation. In Leckman, J. F. and Cohen, D. J. (eds), *Tourette's Syndrome, Tics, Obsessions Compulsions* 40–52. New York: John Wiley & Sons Inc.

Lees, A. J. (1986) Georges Gilles de la Tourette. The man and his times. *Revue Neurologique* (Paris), **142**(11), 808–16.

Lees, A. J. *et al.* (1984) A clinical study of Gilles de la Tourette Syndrome in the United Kingdom. *Journal of Neurology, Neurosurgery and Psychiatry,* **47**, 1–8.

Leonard, H. L. *et al.* (1992) Tics and Tourette's Disorder: a 2–7 year follow-up of 54 obsessive-compulsive children. *American Journal of Psychiatry,* **149**, 1244–51.

Lethem, J. (2000) *Motherless Brooklyn.* London: Faber and Faber Limited.

Long, E. S. *et al.* (1998) A survey of habit bahaviors exhibited by individuals with mental retardation. *Behavioral Interventions,* **13**(2), 79–89.

Loomans, D. (1996) *Today I am Lovable.* Tiburon, CA: H. J. Kramer Inc.

Mandell, M. (1986) Allergy and Tourette's syndrome. *Annals of Allergy,* **56**, 507–8.

Mason, A. *et al.* (1998) The prevalence of Tourette Syndrome in a mainstream school population. *Developmental Medicine and Child Neurology,* **40**, 292–6.

McHenry, L. C. Jr (1967) Samuel Johnson's tics and gesticulations. *Journal of the History of Medicine,* **22**, 152–8.

Mikkelsen, E. J. *et al.* (1981) School avoidance and social phobia triggered by haloperidol in patients with Tourette's disorder. *American Journal of Psychiatry,* **138**,1572–5.

Mosley, J. and Tew, M. (1999) *Quality Circle Time in the Secondary School.* London: David Fulton Publishers.

Murray, T. J. (1979) Dr Samuel Johnson's movement disorders. *British Medical Journal,* i, 1610–14.

NASEN, (1999) *Policy Document on Inclusion.* Tamworth: The National Association for Special Educational Needs.

Norwich, B. (1999) 'The Connotation of special education labels for professionals in the field', *British Journal of Special Needs,* **26**(4), 179–83.

Office of Her Majesty's Chief Inspector of Schools (OFSTED) (1993) *Achieving Good Behaviour in Schools*. London: HMSO.

Olweus, D. (2000) *Bullying at school*. Oxford: Blackwell.

Overmeyer, S. and Taylor, E. (1999) Principles of treatment for hyperkinetic disorder: practice approaches for the UK. *Journal of Child Psychology and Psychiatry*, **40**(8), 1147–57

Packer, L. E. (1997) 'Social and Educational Resources for Patients with Tourette Syndrome', *Neurological Clinics of North America* **15**(2), 457–71.

Pauls, D. L. *et al.* (1986) Gilles de la Tourette's syndrome and obsessive-compulsive disorder. *Archives of General Psychiatry*, **43**, 1180–82.

Rapp, D. J. (1986) Allergy and Tourette's syndrome. *Annals of Allergy*, **56**, 507.

Rauch, S. L. *et al.* (1995) Neurosurgical treatment of Tourette's syndrome: a critical review. *Comprehensive Psychiatry*, **36**, 141–56.

Riddle, M. A. *et al.* (1988) 'Behavioral Symptoms in Tourette's Syndrome', in Cohen, D. J. *et al.* (eds) *Tourette's Syndrome & Tic Disorders*, 151–62. New York: John Wiley & Sons.

Robertson, M. M. (1989) The Gilles de la Tourette Syndrome: The current status. *British Journal of Psychiatry*, **154**, 147–69

Robertson, M. M. (1994) Annotation: Gilles de la Tourette Syndrome – an update. *Journal of Child Psychology and Psychiatry*, **35**, 597–611.

Robertson, M. M. (1995) The relationship between Gilles de la Tourette Syndrome and obsessive compulsive disorder. *Journal of Serotonin Research*, Suppl **11**, 49–62.

Robertson, M. M. (1996) Tourette syndrome around the world. Key Note Address, USA Tourette Syndrome Association, Burbank, California.

Robertson, M. M. (2000) Tourette Syndrome, associated conditions and the complexities of treatment. *Invited Review*. Brain, **123**, 425–62.

Robertson, M. M. and Gourdie A. (1990) Familial Tourette's Syndrome in a large British pedigree: Associated psychopathology, severity of Tourette Syndrome and potential for linkage analysis. *British Journal of Psychiatry*, **156**, 515–21.

Robertson, M. M. and Eapen, V. (1992) Pharmacologic controversy of CNS drugs in Gilles de la Tourette syndrome. *Clinical Neuropharmacology*, **15**, 408–25.

Robertson, M. M. and Eapen, V. (1996) The National Hospital Interview Schedule for the assessment of Gilles de la Tourette syndrome. *International Journal of Methods in Psychiatric Research*, **6**: 203–26.

Robertson, M. M. and Baron-Cohen, S. (1998) *Tourette Syndrome: The Facts*. Oxford: Oxford University Press.

Robertson, M. M. and Stern J. (2000) Gilles de la Tourette Syndrome: symptomatic treatment based on evidence. *European Child and Adolescent Psychiatry* (in press).

Robertson, M. M. *et al.* (1988) The psychopathology of the Gilles de la Tourette Syndrome: a phenomenological analysis. *British Journal of Psychiatry*, **152**, 383–90.

Robertson, M. M. *et al.* (1989) Self-injurious behaviour and the Gilles de la Tourette Syndrome: a clinical study and review of the literature. *Psychological Medicine*, **19**, 611–25.

Robertson, M. M. *et al.* (1993) The psychopathology of Gilles de la Tourette Syndrome:a controlled study. *British Journal of Psychiatry*, **162**, 114–17.

Robertson, M. M. *et al.* (1997) Personality disorder and psychopathology in Tourette's syndrome: a controlled study. *British Journal of Psychiatry*, **171**, 283–6.

Robertson, M. M. *et al.* (1999) The Tourette Syndrome Diagnostic Confidence Index. *Neurology*, **53**, 2108–12.

Roller, J. (1998) 'Facilitating Pupil Involvement in Assessment, Planning and Review Processes', *Educational Psychology in Practice* **13**(4), 266–72.

Sacks, O. (1987) Witty Ticcy Ray. In *The Man Who Mistook his Wife for a Hat* 92–101. New York: Harper and Row.

Sacks, O. (1995) A Surgeon's Life. In *An Anthropologist on Mars* 77–107. New York: Vintage Books; Random House Inc.

Salmon, G. (1998) Bullying in schools: self reported anxiety, depression, and self-esteem in secondary school pupils. *British Medical Journal*, **317**, 924–5.

Santangelo, S. L. *et al.* (1994) Tourette's syndrome: What are the influences of gender and comorbid obsessive-compulsive disorder? *Journal of the American Academy of Child and Adolescent Psychiatry*, **33**, 795–804.

Schultz, R. T. *et al.* (1999) Neuropsychological Findings. In Leckman, J. F. and Cohen, D. J. (eds) *Tourette's Syndrome Tics, Obsessions, Compulsions.* 80–103. New York: John Wiley & Sons Inc.

Shapiro, A. K. *et al.* (1983) Treatment of Gilles de la Tourette syndrome with pimozide. *American Journal of Psychiatry*, **140**, 1183–6.

Shapiro, A. K. *et al.* (1988) *Gilles de la Tourette Syndrome.* New York: Raven Press.

Shimberg, E. F. (1995) *Living with Tourette Syndrome.* New York: Fireside Book; Simon & Schuster.

Simkin, B. (1992) Mozart's scatological disorder. *British Medical Journal*, **305**, (6868), 1563–6.

Stokes, A. *et al.* (1991) Peer Problems in Tourette's Disorder, *Pediatrics*, **87**(6).

Sutherland, R. J. *et al.* (1982) Neuropsychological assessment of children and adults with Tourette syndrome. A comparison with learning disabilities and schizophrenia. *Advances in Neurology*, 35, 311–21.

Swanson, J. M. *et al.* (1998) 'Attention-deficit hyperactivity disorder', *Lancet* **351**, 429–33.

Swedo, S. E. *et al.* (1998) Pediatric autoimmune neuropsychiatric disorders associated with streptococcal infections: clinical description of the first 50 cases. *American Journal of Psychiatry*, **155**, 264–71.

Swerdlow, N. R. (1999) Tourette Syndrome: lessons from a model. *CNS Spectrums*, **4**(3), 16–17.

Thompson, A. J. (1995) Phenylketonuria: an unfolding story. In Robertson, M. M. and Eapen, V. (eds) *Movement and Allied Disorders in Childhood* 83–103. Chichester: John Wiley & Sons.

Tourette Syndrome Association International Consortium for Genetics (1999) A complete genome screen in sib pairs affected by Gilles de la Tourette Syndrome. *American Journal of Human Genetics*, **65**, 1428–36.

Towbin, K. E. *et al.* (1999) Differential Diagnosis. In Leckman, J. F. and Cohen, D. J. (eds) *Tourette's Syndrome, Tics, Obsessions, Compulsions.* 118–139. New York: John Wiley & Sons Inc.

Trinidad, K. and Kurlan, R. (1995) Chorea, athetosis, dystonia, tremor, and parkinsonism. In Robertson, M. M. and Eapen, V. (eds) *Movement and Allied Disorders in Childhood*, 105–47. Chichester: John Wiley & Sons.

Voss, L. D. and Mulligan, J. (2000) Bullying in school; are short pupils at risk? Questionaire study in a cohort. *British Medical Journal*, **320**, 612–13.

Walkup, J. T. (1999) The psychiatry of Tourette Syndrome. *CNS Spectrums*, **4**(2), 54–61.

Walkup, J. T. *et al.* (1992) The validity of instruments measuring tic severity in Tourette's syndrome. *Journal of the American Academy of Child and Adolescent Psychiatry*, **30**(3), 472–7.

Walshe, J. M. (1995) Juvenile Wilson's Disease: The neurological syndrome. In Robertson, M. M. and Eapen, V. (eds) *Movement and Allied Disorders in Childhood*, 69–82. Chichester: John Wiley & Sons.

Waterson, T. (2000) 'Giving guidance on child discipline', *British Medical Journal*, **320**, 261–2.

Wodrich, D. L. *et al.* (1997) Tourette's syndrome and psychopathology in a child psychiatry setting. *Journal of the American Academy of Child and Adolescent Psychiatry*, **36**(1), 1618–24.

Wolff, E. C. (1988) 'Psychotherapeutic Interventions with Tourette's Syndrome', in Cohen, D. J. *et al.* (eds) *Tourette's Syndrome & Tic Disorders*, 207–22. New York: John Wiley & Sons.

World Health Organisation (1992) *International Classification of Diseases and Health Related Problems – Tenth Revision*. Geneva: World Health Organisation.

Index